Mathematics

YEAR 4

Answers

**David Hillard and
Serena Alexander**

GALORE PARK

AN HACHETTE UK COMPANY

About the authors

During his long and distinguished career, David Hillard spent more than 45 years teaching mathematics in two preparatory schools. From 1980 to his retirement, he was associated with the Common Entrance Examination at 11+, 12+ and 13+ levels in the role of adviser, assessor or setter, playing a significant role in the revision of the syllabus in 2003 when the present format of the examination was introduced.

Serena Alexander has taught mathematics since 1987, originally in both maintained and independent senior schools. From 1999 she taught at St Paul's School for Boys, where she was Head of mathematics at their Preparatory School, Colet Court, before moving first to Newton Prep as Deputy Head and more recently to Devonshire House. She is an ISI inspector and helps to run regular mathematics conferences for prep school teachers. She has a passion for maths and expects her pupils to feel the same way. After a lesson or two with her, they normally do!

Every effort has been made to trace all copyright holders, but if any have been inadvertently overlooked, the Publishers will be pleased to make the necessary arrangements at the first opportunity.

Although every effort has been made to ensure that website addresses are correct at time of going to press, Galore Park cannot be held responsible for the content of any website mentioned in this book. It is sometimes possible to find a relocated web page by typing in the address of the home page for a website in the URL window of your browser.

Hachette UK's policy is to use papers that are natural, renewable and recyclable products and made from wood grown in sustainable forests. The logging and manufacturing processes aery effort has re expected to conform to the environmental regulations of the country of origin.

Orders: please contact Bookpoint Ltd, 130 Park Drive, Milton Park, Abingdon, Oxon OX14 4SE. Telephone: (44) 01235 827720. Fax: (44) 01235 400454. Email education@bookpoint.co.uk Lines are open from 9 a.m. to 5 p.m., Monday to Saturday, with a 24-hour message answering service. Visit our website at www.galorepark.co.uk for details of other revision guides for Common Entrance, examination papers and Galore Park publications.

ISBN: 978 1 4718 5648 8

© David Hillard and Serena Alexander 2015

First published in 2015 by

Galore Park Publishing Ltd,

An Hachette UK Company

Carmelite House

50 Victoria Embankment

London EC4Y 0DZ

www.galorepark.co.uk

Impression number   10 9 8 7 6 5 4 3 2 1

Year   2019 2018 2017 2016 2015

All rights reserved. Apart from any use permitted under UK copyright law, no part of this publication may be reproduced or transmitted in any form or by any means, electronic or mechanical, including photocopying and recording, or held within any information storage and retrieval system, without permission in writing from the publisher or under licence from the Copyright Licensing Agency Limited. Further details of such licences (for reprographic reproduction) may be obtained from the Copyright Licensing Agency Limited, Saffron House, 6–10 Kirby Street, London EC1N 8TS.

Illustrations by Aptara, Inc.

Typeset in India

Printed in the UK

A catalogue record for this title is available from the British Library.

Contents

	Introduction	iv
Chapter 1	Place value	1
Chapter 2	More work with numbers	6
Chapter 3	2D shapes	10
Chapter 4	Addition	13
Chapter 5	Subtraction	15
Chapter 6	Addition and subtraction	18
Chapter 7	Position – co-ordinates	20
Chapter 8	Times tables	26
Chapter 9	Multiplication	32
Chapter 10	Division	35
Chapter 11	Symmetry and reflection	38
Chapter 12	Mixed problems	42
Chapter 13	Sequences	44
Chapter 14	Time	46
Chapter 15	Fractions	52
Chapter 16	Calculating with fractions	58
Chapter 17	Fractions and decimals	61
Chapter 18	Calculating with decimals	66
Chapter 19	Metric measurement	69
Chapter 20	Angles and direction	74
Chapter 21	Money	77
Chapter 22	Measurement and scales	80
Chapter 23	Perimeter and area	83
Chapter 24	Tables, charts and graphs	85
	Worksheets	94

Introduction

This book provides a complete set of answers to *Mathematics Year 4 by Galore Park*.

For some questions and activities, pupils are asked to copy diagrams from the book. They may find tracing paper helpful when doing this. Such activities are also supported by separate worksheets which are at the back of this book. These worksheets may be copied.

Place value

This chapter follows the following elements of the National Curriculum for Year 4:
Number - Number and place value

Programme of study (statutory requirements)
Pupils should be taught to:
- recognise the place value of each digit in a four-digit number (thousands, hundreds, tens, and ones)
- identify numbers
- count backwards through zero to include negative numbers
- read Roman numerals to 100 (I to C) and know that over time, the numeral system changed to include the concept of zero and place value.

Notes and guidance (non-statutory)
- Using a variety of representations, pupils become fluent in the order and place value of numbers beyond 1000, including counting in tens and hundreds, and maintaining fluency in other multiples through varied and frequent practice.
- Roman numerals should be put in their historical context so pupils understand that there have been different ways to write whole numbers and that the important concepts of zero and place value were introduced over a period of time.

■ Notes

■ Although pupils are not expected to calculate in millions in Year 4, a million is an interesting number and a good place to start as you introduce larger numbers.

Exercise 1.1 Place value and larger numbers

1. 4000
2. 200 000
3. 10 000
4. 2000
5. 700
6. 30
7. 100 000
8. 9
9. 70 000
10. 400
11. 6
12. 20 000
13. 3000
14. 50
15. 100 000

Exercise 1.2 Writing larger numbers in numerals

1. 3649
2. 8320
3. 1202
4. 5857
5. 7000
6. 3105
7. 9890
8. 3501
9. 8600
10. 3003
11. 18 348
12. 73 901
13. 99 919
14. 40 000
15. 420 600
16. 807 090
17. 324 206
18. 208 300
19. 500 050
20. 660 006

Exercise 1.3 Writing larger numbers in words

1. Four thousand, one hundred and twenty-five
2. One thousand, seven hundred and thirty-two
3. Five thousand, nine hundred and eighty-one
4. Seven thousand, one hundred and thirty-eight
5. Three thousand, six hundred and forty
6. Six thousand and twenty-seven
7. One thousand, five hundred
8. Five thousand and fifty
9. Eighty-four thousand, three hundred and eighty-six
10. Sixty-two thousand, three hundred and seventy-two
11. One hundred and seventy-two thousand, nine hundred and thirty-four
12. Fifty-one thousand, two hundred and seventy-five
13. Twelve thousand, six hundred
14. Seventy-five thousand and twenty
15. Forty-three thousand and ten
16. Eight hundred and forty-two thousand, four hundred and ninety-seven
17. One hundred and sixty-two thousand, five hundred and thirty-four
18. Two hundred and forty-three thousand and twenty
19. Two hundred thousand, one hundred and sixty
20. One hundred and one thousand and ten

Exercise 1.4 Counting in tens

1.
   (a) 72, 82, 92, 102, 112, 122, 132
   (b) 160, 170, 180, 190, 200, 210, 220
   (c) 285, 295, 305, 315, 325, 335, 345
   (d) 1640, 1650, 1660, 1670, 1680, 1690, 1700
   (e) 3600, 3610, 3620, 3630, 3640, 3650, 3660
   (f) 2215, 2225, 2235, 2245, 2255, 2265, 2275

2. (a) 94 (b) 133 (c) 227 (d) 324 (e) 1881 (f) 1010

3.
   (a) 92, 82, 72, 62, 52, 42, 32
   (b) 130, 120, 110, 100, 90, 80, 70
   (c) 217, 207, 197, 187, 177, 167, 157
   (d) 1030, 1020, 1010, 1000, 990, 980, 970
   (e) 6700, 6690, 6680, 6670, 6660, 6650, 6640
   (f) 3425, 3415, 3405, 3395, 3385, 3375, 3365

4. (a) 21 (b) 53 (c) 286 (d) 3679 (e) 5257 (f) 4580

Exercise 1.5 Counting in hundreds

1. (a) 850, 950, 1050, 1150, 1250, 1350, 1450
   (b) 1700, 1800, 1900, 2000, 2100, 2200, 2300
   (c) 2870, 2970, 3070, 3170, 3270, 3370, 3470
   (d) 3694, 3794, 3894, 3994, 4094, 4194, 4294
   (e) 9860, 9960, 10 060, 10 160, 10 260, 10 360, 10 460
   (f) 8292, 8392, 8492, 8592, 8692, 8792, 8892
2. (a) 859 (b) 1443 (c) 2300 (d) 3041 (e) 8095 (f) 5282
3. (a) 1200, 1100, 1000, 900, 800, 700, 600
   (b) 3700, 3600, 3500, 3400, 3300, 3200, 3100
   (c) 4100, 4000, 3900, 3800, 3700, 3600, 3500
   (d) 2552, 2452, 2352, 2252, 2152, 2052, 1952
   (e) 10 300, 10 200, 10 100, 10 000, 9900, 9800, 9700
   (f) 1090, 990, 890, 790, 690, 590, 490
4. (a) 478 (b) 400 (c) 1800 (d) 2950 (e) 11 500 (f) 10 100

Exercise 1.6 Counting in thousands

1. (a) 7000, 8000, 9000, 10 000, 11 000, 12 000, 13 000
   (b) 14 700, 15 700, 16 700, 17 700, 18 700, 19 700, 20 700
   (c) 96 200, 97 200, 98 200, 99 200, 100 200, 101 200, 102 200
   (d) 346 000, 347 000, 348 000, 349 000, 350 000, 351 000, 352 000
   (e) 500 000, 501 000, 502 000, 503 000, 504 000, 505 000, 506 000
   (f) 800 000, 801 000, 802 000, 803 000, 804 000, 805 000, 806 000
2. (a) 9456 (b) 13 870 (c) 15 700 (d) 59 580 (e) 43 230 (f) 46 500
3. (a) 9000, 8000, 7000, 6000, 5000, 4000, 3000
   (b) 27 000, 26 000, 25 000, 24 000, 23 000, 22 000, 21 000
   (c) 81 500, 80 500, 79 500, 78 500, 77 500, 76 500, 75 500
   (d) 100 000, 99 000, 98 000, 97 000, 96 000, 95 000, 94 000
   (e) 810 700, 809 700, 808 700, 807 700, 806 700, 805 700, 804 700
   (f) 30 500, 29 500, 28 500, 27 500, 26 500, 25 500, 24 500
4. (a) 2650 (b) 4350 (c) 14 900 (d) 37 060 (e) 81 500 (f) 9650

Exercise 1.7 Counting through zero

1	4	3	2	1	0	-1	-2	-3	-4		
2	6	-5	-4	-3	-2	-1	0	1	2		
3	8	7	6	5	4	3	2	1	0	-1	-2
4	-5	-4	-3	-2	-1	0	1	2	3	4	5
5	1	0	-1	-2	-3	-4	-5	-6	-7		
6	-9	-8	-7	-6	-5	-4	-3	-2	-1	0	1
7	6	4	2	0	-2	-4	-6	-8			
8	-10	-8	-6	-4	-2	0	2				
9	8	6	4	2	0	-2	-4	-6	-8	-10	-12
10	-5	-3	-1	1	3	5	7	9	11	13	15
11	15	10	5	0	-5	-10	-15				
12	-10	-5	0	5	10	15	20				
13	15	10	5	0	-5	-10	-15	-20	-25	-30	-35
14	-35	-30	-25	-20	-15	-10	-5	0	5	10	15
15	30	20	10	0	-10	-20	-30				
16	-50	-40	-30	-20	-10	0	10	20	30		
17	-400	-300	-200	-100	0	100	200	300	400		
18	300	200	100	0	-100	-200	-300	-400	-500		
19	2000	1000	0	-1000	-2000	-3000	-4000	-5000	-6000		
20	-6000	-5000	-4000	-3000	-2000	-1000	0	1000	2000		

Exercise 1.8 Summary

1 (a) 200   (b) 200 000   (c) 70 000   (d) 8000

2 (a) Twenty-four thousand, three hundred and ten

   (b) One hundred and three thousand and five

   (c) Negative forty-five

3 (a) 15 234   (b) 302 016   (c) -303

4	3750	3760	3770	3780	3790	3800	3810	
5	4132	4122	4112	4102	4092	4082	4072	
6	1600	1700	1800	1900	2000	2100	2200	
7	9350	9250	9150	9050	8950	8850	8750	
8	86 000	87 000	88 000	89 000	90 000	91 000	92 000	
9	4	3	2	1	0	-1	-2	-3	-4	-5	-6
10	-7	-6	-5	-4	-3	-2	-1	0	1	2	3

1 Place value

11	25	20	15	10	5	0	⁻5	⁻10	⁻15
12	400	300	200	100	0	⁻100	⁻200	⁻300	⁻400

13 330   14 5100   15 1650   16 11070

Activity – Roman numerals

Do teach your pupils more about the history of numbers. This is a good opportunity for some cross curricular work. What coins did the Romans use? What number system did the Arabs use? What number system did the Chinese use?

1 X   XX   XXX   XL   L   LX   LXX   LXXX   XC   X

2 (a) XXI   (f) XXVII   3 (a) 7   (f) 45
   (b) XXXV   (g) XLIV   (b) 12   (g) 88
   (c) LXII   (h) XCIX   (c) 22   (h) 79
   (d) LXXIII   (i) CXX   (d) 90   (i) 150
   (e) XCV   (j) CXXXIV   (e) 91

4 CCCLXXXVIII (388)

5 CD (400)   D (500)   M (1000)

1 Place value

2 More work with numbers

This chapter follows the following elements of the National Curriculum for Year 4:
Number - Number and place value

Programme of study (statutory requirements)
Pupils should be taught to:
- order and compare numbers beyond 1000
- identify, represent and estimate numbers using different representations
- round any number to the nearest 10, 100 or 1000
- solve number and practical problems that involve all of the above and with increasingly large positive numbers

Notes and guidance (non-statutory)
- Using a variety of representations, pupils become fluent in the order and place value of numbers beyond 1000, including counting in tens and hundreds, and maintaining fluency in other multiples through varied and frequent practice.

■ Notes

■ This chapter builds on place value to cover ordering, rounding and estimating.

Exercise 2.1 Ordering numbers

1. (a) 974 > 841
   (b) 1483 < 2316
   (c) 5142 > 4901
   (d) 8569 < 8635
   (e) 5839 < 5893
   (f) 6733 > 6730
   (g) 26 481 < 26 841
   (h) 342 168 > 341 168
   (i) 123 456 < 231 546
   (j) 109 384 < 109 386

2. (a) 38, 954, 1528
   (b) 2816, 3217, 4210
   (c) 7019, 7842, 7916
   (d) 1480, 1486, 1489, 1490
   (e) 48 208, 48 219, 48 223
   (f) 23 186, 23 816, 59 234, 59 324
   (g) 349 862, 421 963, 583 206
   (h) 2943, 83 251, 83 260, 106 300, 113 250
   (i) 72 400, 72 411, 72 417, 72 471, 72 477
   (j) 52 014, 52 104, 52 140, 52 410, 521 004

3 (a) 7165   6715   5761   1567
   (b) 8643   8634   3486   3468
   (c) 20 873   18 492   9479
   (d) 59 723   41 685   40 175
   (e) 39 568   38 700   37 392
   (f) 73 291   73 146   73 037
   (g) 34 512   34 125   12 543   12 345
   (h) 143 209   42 185   27 486   4819   4637
   (i) 87 348   87 329   87 175   87 142 87 064
   (j) 643 621   643 612 643 216 643 162 643 126

Exercise 2.2 Ordering with negative numbers

1 (a) 4 is less than 7
   (b) ⁻4 is greater than ⁻8
   (c) ⁻1 is greater than ⁻6
   (d) 5 is greater than ⁻2
   (e) 0 is greater than ⁻8
   (f) 9 is greater than 7
   (g) 9 is greater than ⁻7
   (h) ⁻7 is less than 9
   (i) 7 is less than 9

2 (a) ⁻2 < 0
   (b) 4 > ⁻2
   (c) ⁻3 > ⁻5
   (d) ⁻4 < ⁻1
   (e) 8 > ⁻8
   (f) ⁻7 < ⁻3
   (g) 3 < 7
   (h) ⁻7 < 3
   (i) ⁻3 > ⁻7

3 (a) True   (b) False   (c) False   (d) True   (e) True   (f) True

4 (a) ⁻2   3   4
   (b) ⁻7   6   7
   (c) ⁻5   ⁻4   4
   (d) ⁻2   0   2
   (e) ⁻6   ⁻3   ⁻1
   (f) 1   2   5   6
   (g) ⁻6   ⁻5   ⁻2   ⁻1
   (h) ⁻8   ⁻1   1   4
   (i) ⁻1   0   1   2
   (j) ⁻2   ⁻1   0   2

5 (a) 5   2   ⁻3
   (b) ⁻1   ⁻6   ⁻8
   (c) 5   3   ⁻4
   (d) 1   0   ⁻1
   (e) 4   ⁻2   ⁻4
   (f) 7   4   2   1
   (g) ⁻1   ⁻2   ⁻4   ⁻7
   (h) 8   5   ⁻6   ⁻7
   (i) 9   4   0   ⁻8
   (j) 2   1   ⁻1   ⁻2

Exercise 2.3 Rounding numbers

1 (a) 40   (b) 70   (c) 60   (d) 350   (e) 1040   (f) 6350
2 (a) 200   (b) 500   (c) 400   (d) 1300   (e) 3700   (f) 6400
3 (a) 3000   (b) 4000   (c) 7000   (d) 8000   (e) 2000   (f) 16 000
4 (a) 3000   (b) 11 000 (c) 28 000 (d) 25 000   (e) 147 000   (f) 325 000
5 4000 miles   7 9000 metres   9 4500
6 8000 votes   8 4000 days   10 7499

Exercise 2.4 Estimating and approximating

1 200 children   5 3200 turkeys   9 49 bags
2 450 children   6 32 000 people   10 45 pairs of twins
3 £200   7 22 boxes   11–15 *Check pupils' estimates*
4 £6000   8 19 presents

Exercise 2.5 Problem solving

1 (a) 973   (b) 379
2 (a) 24, 25, 42, 45, 52, 54   (b) 245, 254, 425, 452, 524, 542
3 (a) 1456   (b) 1000   (c) 9865   (d) 10 000
4 (a) 3005   (b) 3000   (c) 9753   (d) 10 000
5 (a) Yate, Yateley, Yatton, Yarwell
   (b) Yarwell 300   Yate 30 000   Yateley 15 000   Yatton 7000
6 (a) 46 499   (b) 45 500
7 15 tubes
8 F   W   Tu   Th   Sa   M   Su

Exercise 2.6 Summary

1 (a) 421 500   421 000   42 199
   (b) 43 100   43 000   34 160
   (c) 109 347   109 345   109 342   109 340
2 (a) 327   783   1891
   (b) 4823   4832   9167   9176
   (c) 127 378   127 387   127 783   127 873
3 (a) ⁻2 < 0   (b) 6 > ⁻3   (c) ⁻4 < ⁻1   (d) ⁻6 > ⁻8
4 (a) 1   0   ⁻2   ⁻6
   (b) 3   ⁻2   ⁻4   ⁻8

5 (a) ⁻6   ⁻4   ⁻1   3
  (b) ⁻4   ⁻2   1   3
6 (a) 40   (b) 70   (c) 80   (d) 20
7 (a) 100   (b) 500   (c) 900   (d) 300
8 (a) 8000   (b) 6000   (c) 9000   (d) 4000
9 Manchester 500 000   Manfield 300   Mannings Heath 1000 or 1100
  Manningtree 5700
10 (a) 8642
   (b) 2468
   (c) 2468 2486 2648 2684 2846 2864 4268 4286 4628 4682
       4826 4862 6248 6284 6428 6482 6824 6842 8246 8264
       8426 8462 8624 8642

Activity – The place value game

Practical.

This very simple game really helps develop pupils' understanding of place value. You can encourage your most able pupils to develop variations of the game:

- Using more digits
- Rolling a die to generate digits
- Using playing cards to generate digits 1-9 and use jokers for 0

3) 2D shapes

This chapter follows the following elements of the National Curriculum for Year 4:

Geometry - Properties of shapes

Programme of study (statutory requirements)
Pupils should be taught to:
- compare and classify geometric shapes, including quadrilaterals and triangles, based on their properties and sizes

Notes and guidance (non-statutory)
- Pupils continue to classify shapes using geometrical properties, extending to classifying different triangles (e.g. isosceles, equilateral, scalene) and quadrilaterals (e.g. parallelogram, rhombus, trapezium).
- Pupils compare lengths and angles to decide if a polygon is regular or irregular.

This chapter also covers the following elements not listed in the National Curriculum programme of study KS2
- Diagonals

■ Notes

■ Pupils are introduced to using a pair of compasses in this chapter. Give them plenty of opportunities to practise.

Exercise 3.1 Circles and semicircles

Pupils should use triangular and square dotted paper and a pair of compasses for this exercise. You may wish to have some circles for pupils to draw round if they are struggling with their compasses.
1–3   *Check pupils' drawings*

Exercise 3.2 Triangles

Pupils should use triangular and square dotted paper for this exercise.
1 *Check pupils' drawings of:*

   (a) *a scalene triangle*   (d) *an obtuse-angled triangle that is not isosceles*

   (b) *an equilateral triangle*   (e) *an obtuse-angled triangle that is isosceles.*

   (c) *an isosceles triangle*

2 *Check pupils' drawings of:*

   (a) *a scalene triangle*   (d) *an obtuse-angled triangle that is not isosceles*

   (b) *a right-angled triangle that is not isosceles* (e) *an obtuse-angled triangle that is isosceles.*

   (c) *a right-angled triangle that is isosceles*

3 *Check pupils' drawings*

Exercise 3.3 Quadrilaterals

Pupils should use triangular and square dotted paper for this exercise.

1 *Check pupils' drawings of:*
   (a) a square – 4 equal sides and 2 pairs of parallel sides marked
   (b) a rectangle – 2 pairs of equal sides and 2 pairs of parallel sides marked
   (c) a trapezium – 1 pair of parallel sides marked

2 *Check pupils' drawings of:*
   (a) a parallelogram – 2 pairs of equal sides and 2 pairs of parallel sides marked
   (b) a rhombus – 4 equal sides and 2 pairs of parallel sides marked
   (c) an arrowhead – 2 pairs of (adjacent) equal sides marked
   (d) an isosceles trapezium – 1 pair of equal sides and 1 pair of parallel sides marked

3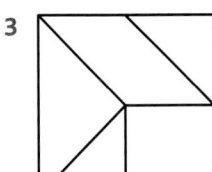

Exercise 3.4 Polygons

1 (a) parallelogram (b) arrowhead (c) pentagon

2 *Check pupils' drawings of:*
   (a) a hexagon   (b) an octagon

3 (a) a square (b) an isosceles triangle (c) an isosceles trapezium (d) a scalene triangle

4 equilateral

5 when all its sides are equal and all its angles are equal

6 10 sides

7 an octagon

8 the same distance apart for the whole length

9 Because it has only one curved side; a polygon has three or more straight sides.

10 (a) 2
   (b) square   rectangle
   (c) square   rhombus   kite
   (d) square   rectangle   rhombus   parallelogram

Activity – Diagonals

1 and 2

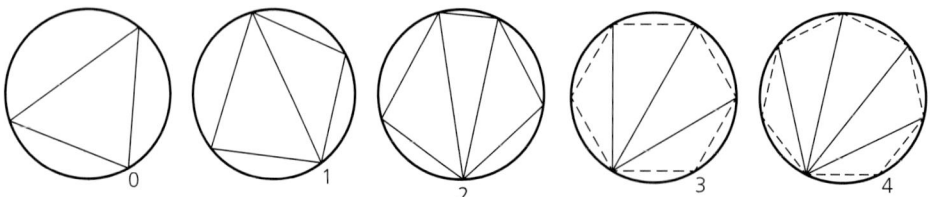

3

Shape	Number of Sides	Number of vertices	Number of diagonals from one vertex
Triangle	3	3	0
Quadrilateral	4	4	1
Pentagon	5	5	2
Hexagon	6	6	3
Heptagon	7	7	4

4 The number of diagonals from one vertex is 3 less than the number of sides/vertices.

    (a) A hexagon has 3 diagonals from one vertex.

    (b) An octagon has 5 diagonals.

    (c) A 50-sided figure has 47 diagonals from one vertex.

5 The number of diagonals from one vertex is 3 less than the number of sides/vertices.

Shape	Sides	Number of diagonals from one vertex	Total number of diagonals
Triangle	3	0	0
(a) Quadrilateral	4	1	2
(b) Pentagon	5	2	5
(c) Hexagon	6	3	9
(d) Octagon	8	5	20

Addition

This chapter follows the following elements of the National Curriculum for Year 4:

Number - Number and place value

Programme of study (statutory requirements)
Pupils should be taught to:
- find 1000 more or less than a given number

Number-Addition and subtraction

Programme of study (statutory requirements)
Pupils should be taught to:
- add and subtract numbers with up to 4 digits using the formal written methods of columnar addition and subtraction where appropriate
- solve addition and subtraction problems in contexts

Notes and guidance (non-statutory)
- Pupils continue to practise both mental methods and columnar addition with increasingly large numbers to aid fluency.

■ Notes

■ Although there should be a focus on sound mental calculation, it is important to stress that there is no one correct method. Encourage pupil discussion and give them lots of practice.

Exercise 4.1 Mental addition

1	1100	10	12 900	19	6460	28	1402
2	1400	11	13 000	20	8760	29	924
3	6000	12	12 700	21	13 740	30	1215
4	16 000	13	4970	22	11 930	31	1812
5	7900	14	6880	23	17 010	32	620
6	6800	15	8000	24	18 600	33	2598
7	8500	16	9100	25	14 050	34	3010
8	4200	17	5630	26	10 450	35	9000
9	8500	18	8970	27	14 250	36	20 000

Exercise 4.2 Formal addition

| 1 | 598 | 3 | 3487 | 5 | 1968 | 7 | 3901 |
| 2 | 478 | 4 | 592 | 6 | 2556 | 8 | 3933 |

9	2868	15	4243	21	3113	27	8831
10	4735	16	521	22	4325	28	5124
11	2833	17	1404	23	7412	29	3747
12	3344	18	3240	24	5223	30	7839
13	4302	19	5233	25	5080		
14	5000	20	6194	26	4593		

Exercise 4.3 Problem solving

1 263 cows and sheep 4 1852 7 6918 miles 10 78 227 people
2 183 miles 5 2274 runs 8 8138 items
3 2642 books 6 5007 people 9 2838 people

Exercise 4.4 Summary

1 (a) 1200 (b) 780 (c) 9500 (d) 7000 (e) 885 (f) 3620
2 (a) 589 (b) 1563 (c) 4370 (d) 2346 (e) 3640 (f) 6852
3 1453   4 2352 pupils   5 8675 items

Activity – Magic squares

2	7	6
9	5	1
4	3	8

1 Each vertical, horizontal or diagonal line has a total of 15, which is three times the number in the centre.
2 For those lines which pass through the centre, the numbers either side of 5 need to be 5 +/− the same difference, to give a total of 15

Using only the numbers 1 to 9, the four lines with 5 at the centre must be:

1 5 9
2 5 8
3 5 7
4 5 6

These lines can be arranged in different ways. Remember that the four outer lines must also add up to 15
For example:

8	3	4
1	5	9
6	7	2

4	3	8
9	5	1
2	7	6

8	1	6
3	5	7
4	9	2

3 Pupils' comments

5 Subtraction

This chapter follows the following elements of the National Curriculum for Year 4:
Number - Addition and subtraction

Programme of study (statutory requirements)
Pupils should be taught to:
- estimate and use inverse operations to check answers to a calculation
- add and subtract numbers with up to 4 digits using the formal written methods of columnar addition and subtraction where appropriate
- solve addition and subtraction problems in contexts

Notes and guidance (non-statutory)
- Pupils continue to practise both mental methods and columnar subtraction with increasingly large numbers to aid fluency.

■ Notes

■ Encourage discussion on the various methods and strategies for subtracting mentally and give pupils plenty of practice.

Exercise 5.1 Mental strategies

1   63
2   55
3   371
4   108
5   218
6   1051
7   1732
8   901
9   1295
10 320
11 220
12 210
13 460
14 260
15 2510
16 1420
17 2670
18 5441
19 107
20 255
21 244
22 435
23 147
24 1165
25 8690
26 3408
27 3205

Exercise 5.2 Formal written methods

1   212
2   315
3   332
4   282
5   225
6   1011
7   4351
8   3444
9   7140
10 2214
11 5330
12 6161
13 6230
14 3121
15 5237
16 2015
17 5004
18 3142

Exercise 5.3 Subtraction with decomposition

1 138
2 256
3 355
4 173
5 469
6 1667
7 2377
8 637
9 657
10 1177
11 3268
12 1738
13 749
14 2808
15 2776
16 1487
17 462
18 2208

Exercise 5.4 Subtracting from numbers with zeros

1 227
2 273
3 218
4 227
5 273
6 218
7 319
8 555
9 2322
10 1527
11 2053
12 6121
13 1314
14 2121
15 2136
16 4116
17 186
18 5378

Exercise 5.5 Subtraction with borrowing

1 307
2 321
3 233
4 244
5 281
6 308
7 331
8 505
9 2375
10 647
11 1647
12 5099
13 1575
14 2892
15 2953
16 3957
17 1192
18 96

Exercise 5.6 Problem solving

1 48 plain digestive biscuits
2 39 miles
3 145
4 503 pages
5 52 years old
6 1758
7 857 seats
8 85 points
9 3552 miles
10 12 941

Exercise 5.7 Summary

1 14
2 44
3 5
4 107
5 106
6 404
7 877
8 313
9 1995
10 4750
11 1263
12 2746
13 4595
14 3255
15 237
16 576
17 680
18 1166
19 575
20 366 m
21 1218 more apples
22 64 years
23 1143 umbrellas
24 7495 visitors

Activity – Magic squares revisited

1
9	2	7
4	6	8
5	10	3

3
11	4	9
6	8	10
7	12	5

5
15	8	13
10	12	14
11	16	9

2
10	3	8
5	7	9
6	11	4

4
12	5	10
7	9	11
8	13	6

Patterns of magic squares

Each line totals three times the number in the centre.

The difference between the number in the centre and the numbers on either side of it is the same. For example, in the magic square in question 5, the top left to bottom right diagonal has a centre of 12 and the difference either side is 3

12 + 3 = 15   and   12 – 3 = 9

1 Total is 6 × 3 = 18

5	6	7	(–/+1)
4	6	8	(–/+2)
3	6	9	(–/+3)
2	6	10	(–/+4)

3 Total is 8 × 3 = 24

7	8	9	(–/+1)
6	8	10	(–/+2)
5	8	11	(–/+3)
4	8	12	(–/+4)

2 Total is 7 × 3 = 21

6	7	8	(–/+1)
5	7	9	(–/+2)
4	7	10	(–/+3)
3	7	11	(–/+4)

4 Total is 9 × 3 = 27

8	9	10	(–/+1)
7	9	11	(–/+2)
6	9	12	(–/+3)
5	9	13	(–/+4)

The numbers above can be written in this order:

- diagonally, from bottom left to top right
- across the middle from left to right
- diagonally, from bottom right to top left
- down the middle from top to bottom.

6 Addition and subtraction

This chapter follows the following elements of the National Curriculum for Year 4:

Number - Addition and subtraction

Programme of study (statutory requirements)
Pupils should be taught to:
- estimate and use inverse operations to check answers to a calculation
- solve addition and subtraction two-step problems in contexts, deciding which operations and methods to use and why

Notes and guidance (non-statutory)
- Pupils continue to practise both mental methods and columnar addition and subtraction with increasingly large numbers to aid fluency.

Exercise 6.1 Addition and subtraction

1. 92
2. 38
3. 136
4. 98
5. 50
6. 12
7. 89
8. 47
9. 109
10. 179
11. 217
12. 536
13. 258
14. 531
15. 184
16. 1450
17. 583
18. 2936
19. 6523
20. 1081

Exercise 6.2 Inverses

1. 9 + **3** = 12
2. 11 + **9** = 20
3. 25 − **6** = 19
4. 31 − 6 = **25**
5. 25 + 6 = **31**
6. 18 + 24 = **42**
7. 42 − **18** = 24
8. 42 − **24** = 18
9. 116 − **52** = 64
10. 52 + 64 = **116**
11. 282 + **222** = 504
12. 738 − **395** = 343
13. 250 + 170 = **420**
14. 472 − 160 = **312**
15. 417 + **303** = 720
16. 2450 − 1200 = **1250**
17. 8570 − 7085 = **1485**
18. 825 + 975 = **1800**

Exercise 6.3 Problem solving

1. 13 children
2. 82 marbles
3. 33 exercise books
4. (a) No
   (b) 13 short
5. 192 newspapers
6. 446 loaves
7. 66 marks
8. No, he scores 494
9. 1072 passengers
10. 3432 passengers

Exercise 6.4 Summary

1 (a) 58 (b) 24 (c) 100 (d) 37

2 (a) 43 + **11** = 54 (e) 35 + 27 + **48** = 110 (i) 125 + 33 − **90** = 68
  (b) 140 − **67** = 73 (f) 58 + **68** − 46 = 80 (j) 40 − 30 − **10** = 0
  (c) **225** − 80 = 145 (g) **75** − 12 − 38 = 25
  (d) **65** + 80 = 145 (h) 70 − 47 + **37** = 60

3 113 fish fingers   4 305 passengers   5 Austen House has 1049 house points.

Activity – Missing digits

1
T	U
3	4
+ 2	3
5	7

4
Th	H	T	U
	4	**6**	3
+	9	3	7
1	4	0	0

7
H	T	U
8	5	**4**
− 2	1	9
6	3	5

2
H	T	U
	7	4
+	4	9
1	2	3

5
T	U
9	6
− 7	**1**
2	5

8
H	T	U
8	4	1
− **1**	**9**	**6**
6	4	5

3
H	T	U
1	3	6
+	**6**	**2**
1	9	8

6
H	T	U
6	**0**	7
− **2**	4	5
3	6	**2**

Position – co-ordinates

This chapter follows the following elements of the National Curriculum for Year 4:

Geometry - Position and direction

Programme of study (statutory requirements)
Pupils should be taught to:
- describe positions on a 2D grid as co-ordinates in the first quadrant
- plot specified points and draw sides to complete a given polygon
- describe movements between positions as translations of a given unit to the left/right and up/down

Notes and guidance (non-statutory)
- Pupils draw a pair of axes in one quadrant, with equal scales and integer labels.
- They read, write and use pairs of co-ordinates (2, 5)

■ Notes

■ Pupils should be given the opportunity to draw and label their own axes, mark scales on both axes and label the origin.

Exercise 7.1 Grids and co-ordinates

A (1, 2)   C (4, 7)   E (7, 6)   G (5, 3)   I (0, 1)
B (2, 4)   D (6, 8)   F (8, 1)   H (3, 5)   J (1, 0)

Exercise 7.2 Other scales

A (2, 8)   C (5, 4)   E (6, 0)   G (1, 2)   I (5, 7)
B (4, 5)   D (7, 3)   F (3, 1)   H (0, 7)   J (8, 6)

Exercise 7.3 Plotting points

1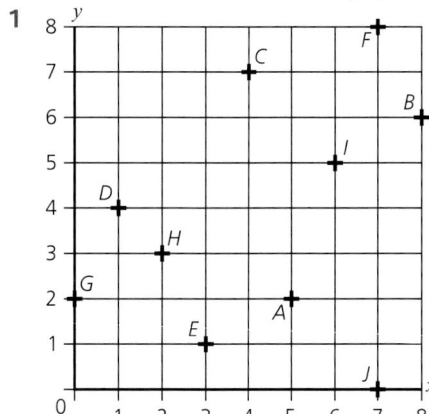

2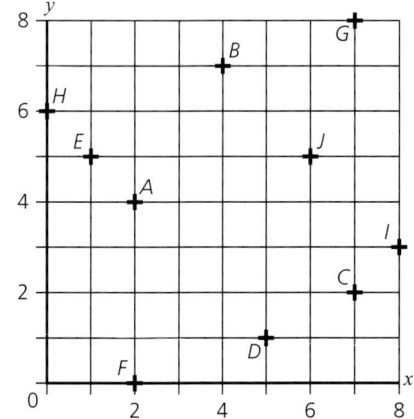

Exercise 7.4 Drawing shapes
1–4

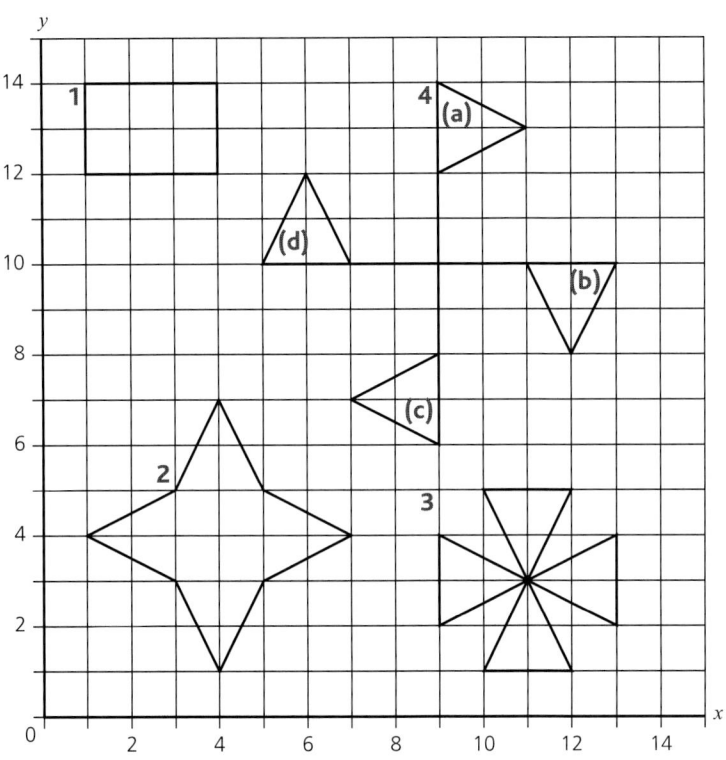

Exercise 7.5 Drawing shapes with letters
1–3

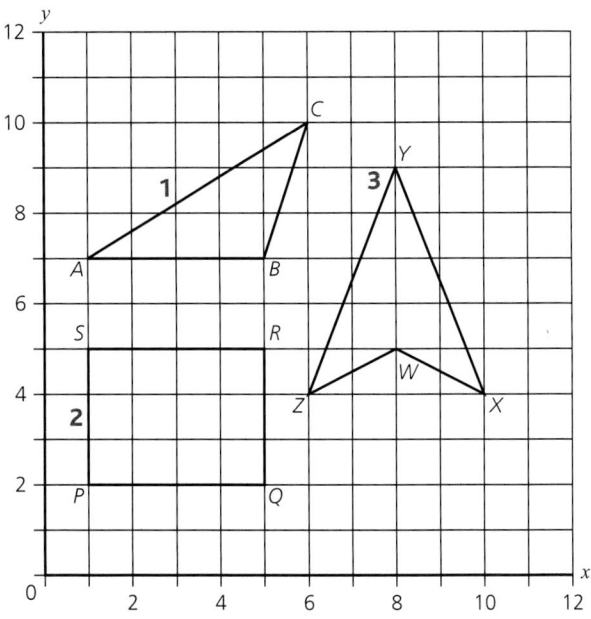

4   ABC = scalene triangle   PQRS = rectangle   WXYZ = arrowhead
5   (a) See grid question 8   (b) an isosceles triangle
6   (a) See grid question 8   (b) a kite   (c) See grid question 8   (d) 90°
7   (a)–(c) See grid question 8   (d) Z(12, 8)
8   (a)–(c) See grid question 8   (d) G(11, 6)

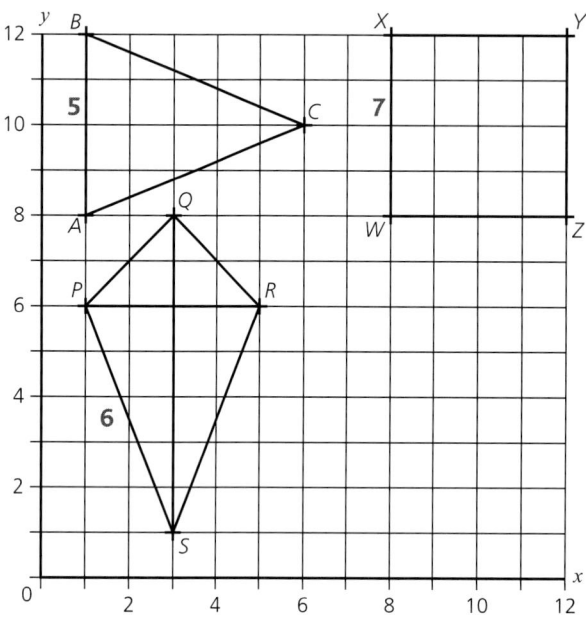

8   (a)–(c) See grid question 9

There are alternate positions for U, but it is likely pupils will draw the shape shown on the grid.

(d) T(8, 8) and U(7, 10) but other answers acceptable.

9   (a)–(c) See grid

There are alternate positions for G and H, but it is likely pupils will draw the shapes shown on the grid.

(d) G(1, 4) and H(1, 6) but other answers are acceptable.

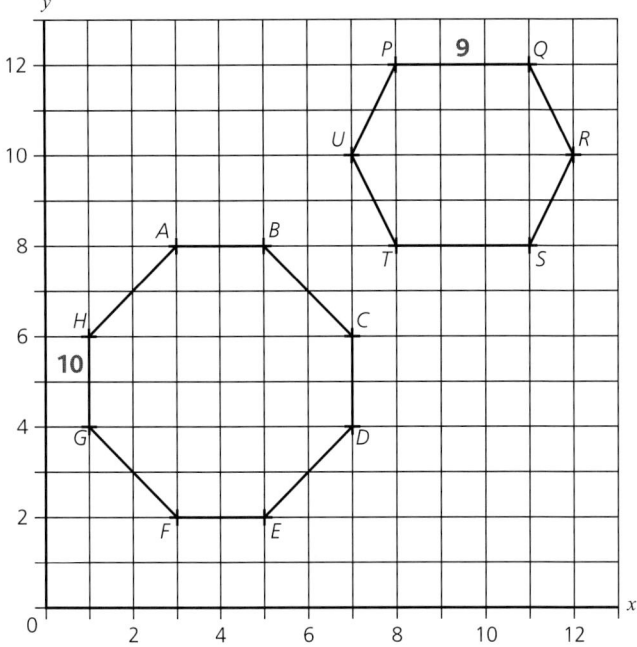

Exercise 7.6 Describing translations

1. (a) 4 units right
   (b) 3 units down
   (c) 3 units right followed by 7 units up
   (d) 5 units left followed by 8 units down
   (e) 1 unit right followed by 5 units up
   (f) 3 units right followed by 1 unit up
   (g) 2 units left followed by 4 units down
   (h) 1 unit right followed by 1 unit down
   (i) 2 units left followed by 4 units up
   (j) 3 units left followed by 7 units down

Exercise 7.7 Drawing translations

1 B(6, 7)
2 D(8, 0)
3 F(5, 5)
4 H(7, 5)
5 K(2, 4)
6 M(6, 0)
7 Q(9, 9)
8 S(3, 4)
9 W(10, 3)
10 X(4, 3)
11 Y(6, 7)
12 Z(6, 0)

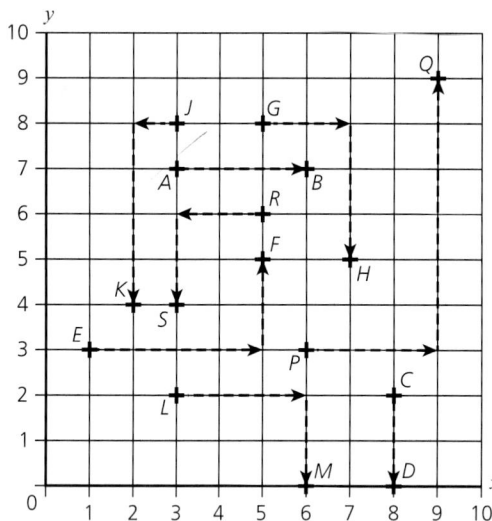

Exercise 7.8 Summary

1 A(3, 7)   B(6, 7)   C(1, 3)   D(8, 4)   E(8, 0)   F(0, 5)

2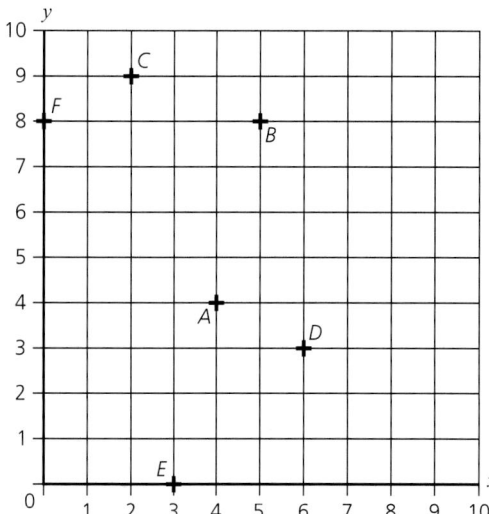

3 (a) See grid question 5
   (b) See grid question 5
   (c) an isosceles right-angled triangle

4 (a) See grid question 5
   (b) See grid question 5
   (c) Rhombus
   (d) Z(7, 2)

5 (a)–(c) See grid question 5
   (d) Z(6, 9)

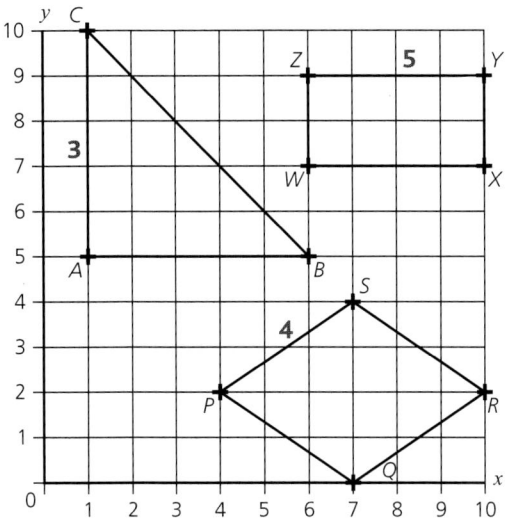

6 (a) 3 units right
   (b) 5 units left followed by 4 units down
   (c) 7 units right followed by 1 unit up
   (d) 4 units down
   (e) 8 units left followed by 5 units up
   (f) 3 units right followed by 2 units up

7 (a) B(4, 5)   (b) D(2, 4)   (c) F(8, 8)   (d) H(4, 0)

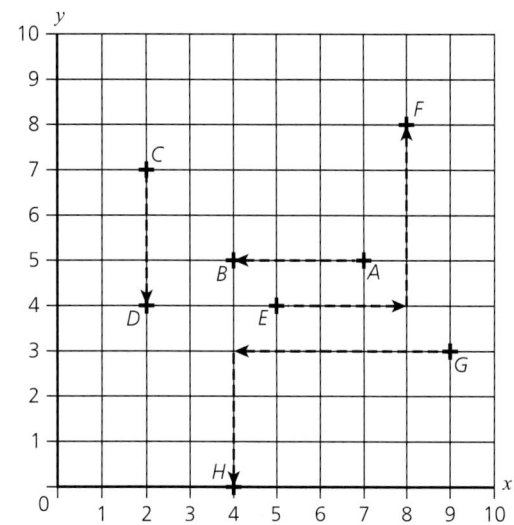

8 (a) X(7, 4)   (b) Y(5, 0)   (c) Z(9, 6)

Activity – Making squares

Check pupils' answers

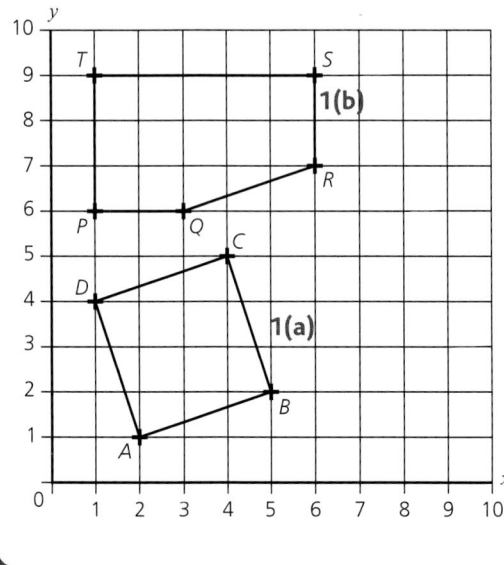

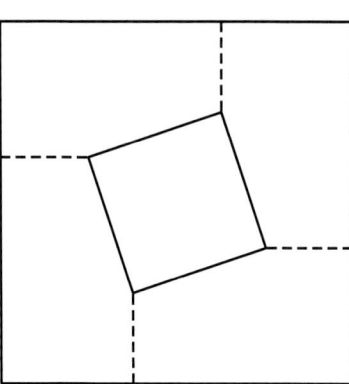

Times tables

This chapter follows the following elements of the National Curriculum for Year 4:

Number - Number and place value

Programme of study (statutory requirements)
Pupils should be taught to:
- count in multiples of 6, 7, 9, 25

Number - Multiplication and division

Programme of study (statutory requirements)
Pupils should be taught to:
- recall multiplication and division facts for multiplication tables up to 12 × 12 (needs to include 0)
- use place value, known and derived facts to multiply and divide mentally, including: multiplying by 0 and 1; dividing by 1; multiplying together three numbers
- recognise and use factor pairs and commutativity in mental calculations

Notes and guidance (non-statutory)
- Pupils continue to practise recalling and using multiplication tables and related division facts to aid fluency.
- Pupils practise mental methods and extend this to three-digit numbers to derive facts, for example 200 × 3 = 600 into 600 ÷ 3 = 200
- Pupils write statements about the equality of expressions (e.g. use the distributive law 39 × 7 = 30 × 7 + 9 × 7 and associative law (2 × 3) × 4 = 2 × (3 × 4)). They combine their knowledge of number facts and rules of arithmetic to solve mental and written calculations e.g. 2 × 6 × 5 = 10 × 6

■ Notes

■ Give pupils plenty of practice with multiplication tables. Some will remember them with ease, but others will need to revisit them frequently, particularly the 7s, 8s, 9s and 12s.

Exercise 8.1 Counting on

This exercise is intended to be done orally as a class activity.

1. 6, 12, 18, 24, 30, 36, 42
2. 7, 14, 21, 28, 35, 42
3. 9, 18, 27, 36, 45, 54
4. 6, 12, 18, 24, 30, 36, 42, 48, 54
5. 6, 12, 18, 24, 30, 36, 42, 48
6. 8, 16, 24, 32, 40, 48
7. 7, 14, 21, 28, 35, 42, 49, 56
8. 8, 16, 24, 32, 40, 48, 56
9. 9, 18, 27, 36, 45, 54, 63
10. 7, 14, 21, 28, 35, 42, 49
11. 8, 16, 24, 32, 40, 48, 56, 64
12. 9, 18, 27, 36, 45, 54, 63, 72
13. 8, 16, 24, 32, 40, 48, 56, 64, 72
14. 9, 18, 27, 36, 45, 54, 63, 72, 81

15 (a) (i) 77   (ii) 84   (b) (i) 88   (ii) 96   (c) (i) 99   (ii) 108
16 (a) 110   (b) 121   (c) 132
17 144   18 25, 50, 75, 100   19 300
20 (a) (i) 36, 27, 18, 9, 0   (iii) 36, 32, 28, 24, 20, 16, 12, 8, 4, 0
 (ii) 36, 30, 24, 18, 12, 6, 0
 (b) (i) 72, 60, 48, 36, 24, 12, 0   (iii) 72, 64, 56, 48, 40, 32, 24, 16, 8, 0
 (ii) 72, 63, 54, 45, 36, 27, 18, 9, 0

Exercise 8.2 Doubling and trebling

1

3 times table	
0 × 3 =	0
1 × 3 =	3
2 × 3 =	6
3 × 3 =	9
4 × 3 =	12
5 × 3 =	15
6 × 3 =	18
7 × 3 =	21
8 × 3 =	24
9 × 3 =	27
10 × 3 =	30
11 × 3 =	33
12 × 3 =	36

6 times table	
0 × 6 =	0
1 × 6 =	6
2 × 6 =	12
3 × 6 =	18
4 × 6 =	24
5 × 6 =	30
6 × 6 =	36
7 × 6 =	42
8 × 6 =	48
9 × 6 =	54
10 × 6 =	60
11 × 6 =	66
12 × 6 =	72

9 times table	
0 × 9 =	0
1 × 9 =	9
2 × 9 =	18
3 × 9 =	27
4 × 9 =	36
5 × 9 =	45
6 × 9 =	54
7 × 9 =	63
8 × 9 =	72
9 × 9 =	81
10 × 9 =	90
11 × 9 =	99
12 × 9 =	108

2

4 times table	
0 × 4 =	0
1 × 4 =	4
2 × 4 =	8
3 × 4 =	12
4 × 4 =	16
5 × 4 =	20
6 × 4 =	24
7 × 4 =	28
8 × 4 =	32
9 × 4 =	36
10 × 4 =	40
11 × 4 =	44
12 × 4 =	48

6 times table	
0 × 6 =	0
1 × 6 =	6
2 × 6 =	12
3 × 6 =	18
4 × 6 =	24
5 × 6 =	30
6 × 6 =	36
7 × 6 =	42
8 × 6 =	48
9 × 6 =	54
10 × 6 =	60
11 × 6 =	66
12 × 6 =	72

12 times table	
0 × 12 =	0
1 × 12 =	12
2 × 12 =	24
3 × 12 =	36
4 × 12 =	48
5 × 12 =	60
6 × 12 =	72
7 × 12 =	84
8 × 12 =	96
9 × 12 =	108
10 × 12 =	120
11 × 12 =	132
12 × 12 =	144

Exercise 8.3 The 7 and 11 times tables

1

7 times table	
0 × 7 =	0
1 × 7 =	7
2 × 7 =	14
3 × 7 =	21
4 × 7 =	28
5 × 7 =	35
6 × 7 =	42
7 × 7 =	49
8 × 7 =	56
9 × 7 =	63
10 × 7 =	70
11 × 7 =	77
12 × 7 =	84

2

11 times table	
0 × 11 =	0
1 × 11 =	11
2 × 11 =	22
3 × 11 =	33
4 × 11 =	44
5 × 11 =	55
6 × 11 =	66
7 × 11 =	77
8 × 11 =	88
9 × 11 =	99
10 × 11 =	110
11 × 11 =	121
12 × 11 =	132

3 and 4 *Shading will differ*

×	1	2	3	4	5	6	7	8	9	10	11	12
1	1	2	3	4	5	6	7	8	9	10	11	12
2	2	4	6	8	10	12	14	16	18	20	22	24
3	3	6	9	12	15	18	21	24	27	30	33	36
4	4	8	12	16	20	24	28	32	36	40	44	48
5	5	10	15	20	25	30	35	40	45	50	55	60
6	6	12	18	24	30	36	42	48	54	60	66	72
7	7	14	21	28	35	42	49	56	63	70	77	84
8	8	16	24	32	40	48	56	64	72	80	88	96
9	9	18	27	36	45	54	63	72	81	90	99	108
10	10	20	30	40	50	60	70	80	90	100	110	120
11	11	22	33	44	55	66	77	88	99	110	121	132
12	12	24	36	48	60	72	84	96	108	120	132	144

Experience tells us that the multiplication bonds children have most difficulty remembering are the ones shaded above. Do revisit these frequently.

Exercise 8.4 Times tables practice

1 24
2 35
3 99
4 48
5 54
6 14
7 121
8 40
9 36
10 96
11 49
12 81
13 110
14 48
15 84
16 64
17 77
18 72
19 63
20 88
21 108
22 42
23 32
24 132
25 45
26 24
27 24
28 144
29 72
30 33

Exercise 8.5 The inverse

6 inverse times table	
0 ÷ 6 =	0
60 ÷ 6 =	10
18 ÷ 6 =	3
72 ÷ 6 =	12
66 ÷ 6 =	11
54 ÷ 6 =	9
6 ÷ 6 =	1
12 ÷ 6 =	2
24 ÷ 6 =	4
48 ÷ 6 =	8
42 ÷ 6 =	7
36 ÷ 6 =	6
30 ÷ 6 =	5

7 inverse times table	
7 ÷ 7 =	1
77 ÷ 7 =	11
21 ÷ 7 =	3
35 ÷ 7 =	5
14 ÷ 7 =	2
42 ÷ 7 =	6
28 ÷ 7 =	4
63 ÷ 7 =	9
70 ÷ 7 =	10
0 ÷ 7 =	0
56 ÷ 7 =	8
84 ÷ 7 =	12
49 ÷ 7 =	7

9 inverse times table	
18 ÷ 9 =	2
45 ÷ 9 =	5
27 ÷ 9 =	3
9 ÷ 9 =	1
36 ÷ 9 =	4
0 ÷ 9 =	0
63 ÷ 9 =	7
90 ÷ 9 =	10
81 ÷ 9 =	9
99 ÷ 9 =	11
72 ÷ 9 =	8
108 ÷ 9 =	12
54 ÷ 9 =	6

11 inverse times table	
22 ÷ 11 =	2
11 ÷ 11 =	1
66 ÷ 11 =	6
55 ÷ 11 =	5
0 ÷ 11 =	0
99 ÷ 11 =	9
33 ÷ 11 =	3
88 ÷ 11 =	8
44 ÷ 11 =	4
121 ÷ 11 =	11
77 ÷ 11 =	7
132 ÷ 11 =	12
110 ÷ 11 =	10

12 inverse times table	
24 ÷ 12 =	2
60 ÷ 12 =	5
12 ÷ 12 =	1
36 ÷ 12 =	3
72 ÷ 12 =	6
0 ÷ 12 =	0
48 ÷ 12 =	4
120 ÷ 12 =	10
96 ÷ 12 =	8
108 ÷ 12 =	9
144 ÷ 12 =	12
84 ÷ 12 =	7
132 ÷ 12 =	11

Exercise 8.6 More times tables practice

1. $2 \times 6 = 12$
2. $4 \times 6 = 24$
3. $36 \div 9 = 4$
4. $99 \div 11 = 9$
5. $8 \times 7 = 56$
6. $11 \times 6 = 66$
7. $12 \times 6 = 72$
8. $6 \times 8 = 48$
9. $49 \div 7 = 7$
10. $132 \div 12 = 11$
11. $6 \times 3 = 18$
12. $27 \div 9 = 3$
13. $45 \div 5 = 9$
14. $5 \times 6 = 30$
15. $7 \times 9 = 63$
16. $28 \div 7 = 4$
17. $12 \times 7 = 84$
18. $54 \div 9 = 6$
19. $7 \times 5 = 35$
20. $6 \times 9 = 54$
21. $72 \div 9 = 8$
22. $88 \div 8 = 11$
23. $9 \times 9 = 81$
24. $108 \div 12 = 9$
25. $11 \times 11 = 121$
26. $132 \div 11 = 12$
27. $8 \times 7 = 56$

Exercise 8.7 Multiplying with larger numbers

1. 60
2. 60
3. 84
4. 120
5. 160
6. 162
7. 280
8. 360
9. 220
10. 240
11. 120
12. 128
13. 216
14. 320
15. 1280
16. 224
17. 600
18. 900

Exercise 8.8 Multiplication by partition

1. 76
2. 147
3. 344
4. 455
5. 390
6. 518
7. 224
8. 153
9. 567
10. 228
11. 354
12. 324
13. 301
14. 174
15. 355
16. 776
17. 243
18. 216

Exercise 8.9 Using the inverse

1. (a) 200 (b) 4 (c) 2
2. (a) 3 (b) 600 (c) 2
3. (a) 90 (b) 5 (c) 9
4. (a) 8 (b) 720 (c) 9
5. (a) 40 (b) 15 (c) 150
6. (a) 4 (b) 640 (c) 40
7. $420 \div 7 = 60$
8. $70 \times 6 = 420$
9. $80 \times 5 = 400$
10. $400 \div 8 = 50$
11. $7 \times 120 = 840$
12. $1440 \div 120 = 12$
13. $120 \times 12 = 1440$
14. $480 \div 40 = 12$
15. $30 \times 4 = 120$
16. $480 \div 60 = 8$
17. $25 \times 24 = 600$
18. $900 \div 25 = 36$

Exercise 8.10 Problem solving

1 84 yoghurts
2 8 packets
3 12 groups
4 96 cartons
5 12 packs
6 192 chairs
7 90 packs
8 360 pages
9 864p = £8.64
10 24 hand basins

Exercise 8.11 Summary

1 (a) 42   (b) 108   (c) 56   (d) 132   (e) 35   (f) 72
2 (a) 5   (b) 7   (c) 12   (d) 11   (e) 12   (f) 9
3 (a) 24   (b) 270   (c) 140   (d) 700   (e) 288   (f) 351
4 (a) 70 × **9** = 630   (b) 720 ÷ **90** = 8   (c) **6** × 70 = 420   (d) 500 ÷ **25** = 20
5 120 bananas   6 50 children   7 5000 house points

> ### Activity – Times table bingo
>
> An enjoyable activity that can be adapted to a range of abilities.
>
> The extension activity involves working out which multiples are more likely to occur. Encourage more able pupils to set up a multiplication square. They should find that 36 and 24 could occur in three different ways and 18 and 48 in two different ways.
>
> More able pupils could be asked to investigate what happens when the numbers on the dice are changed.

9 Multiplication

This chapter follows the following elements of the National Curriculum for Year 4:

Number - Multiplication and division

Programme of study (statutory requirements)
Pupils should be taught to:
- recall multiplication and division facts for multiplication tables up to 12 × 12 (needs to include 0)
- multiply two-digit and three-digit numbers by a one-digit number using formal written layout
- solve problems involving multiplying and adding, including using the distributive law to multiply two digit numbers by one digit, integer scaling problems and harder correspondence problems such as n objects are connected to m objects.

Notes and guidance (non-statutory)
- Pupils practise to become fluent in the formal written method of short multiplication for multiplying using multi-digit numbers, and short division with exact answers when dividing by a one-digit number.
- Pupils solve two-step problems in contexts, choosing the appropriate operation, working with increasingly harder numbers. This should include correspondence questions such as the numbers of choices of a meal on a menu, or three cakes shared equally between 10 children.

■ Notes

■ Many children find the lattice or gelosia multiplication method covered in the end of chapter activity more straightforward than the formal methods, so you could use this as an introduction.

Exercise 9.1 Multiplying by 10, 100 and 1000

1 50	6 81 900	11 25 000	16 5 000 000
2 1350	7 500 000	12 1 780 000	17 6 575 000
3 830	8 7500	13 20 000 000	18 1 000 000
4 40 000	9 345 000	14 382 000	
5 3100	10 500	15 8000	

Exercise 9.2 Square numbers

1 Squares of side length 1, 2, 3, 4, 5, 6, 7, 8, 9 and 10, representing the square numbers 1, 4, 9, 16, 25, 36, 49, 64, 81 and 100

2 A square number is the result of multiplying a number by itself.

Exercise 9.3 The formal method of multiplication

1. 174
2. 138
3. 390
4. 520
5. 148
6. 312
7. 186
8. 567
9. 126
10. 252
11. 329
12. 549
13. 336
14. 375
15. 196
16. 306
17. 92
18. 120
19. 413
20. 114

Exercise 9.4 Multiplying a 3-digit number by a 1-digit number

1. 534
2. 1088
3. 2145
4. 4452
5. 1332
6. 708
7. 5698
8. 2916
9. 1312
10. 2550
11. 3412
12. 2187
13. 2625
14. 2955
15. 1968
16. 5760
17. 4284
18. 4545

Exercise 9.5 Problem solving

1. 288 tennis balls
2. 168 notebooks
3. 324 eggs
4. 384 bottles
5. 300 stamps
6. 720 screws
7. 555 pencils
8. 496 tyres
9. 1435 kg
10. 585 km

Exercise 9.6 Making choices

1. 4 combinations
2. 6 combinations
3. $2 \times 2 \times 2 \times 2 = 16$ ways
4. 12 combinations
5. (a) $2 \times 2 \times 2 = 8$ meals (b) $3 \times 3 \times 3 = 27$ meals
6. $3 \times 3 = 9$ combinations
7. 12 combinations
8. (a) 4 ways (b) 27 ways (c) 256 ways (d) 24 ways

Exercise 9.7 Summary

1. (a) 870
   (b) 2 396 000
   (c) 800
   (d) 45 000
   (e) 56 700
   (f) 10 000
   (g) 69 000
   (h) 650 000
   (i) 4000

2. (a) 255
   (b) 273
   (c) 378
   (d) 424
   (e) 558
   (f) 1872
   (g) 314
   (h) 2492
   (i) 1820

3. 5184 exercise books
4. 432 eggs
5. 20 combinations
6. 12 ways

Activity – Another way to multiply

This method is frequently used in various countries and in some schools.
Many children find it easier than grid multiplication.

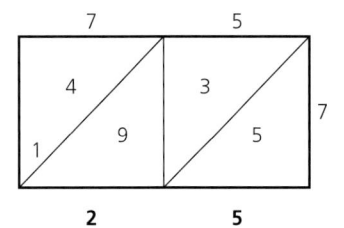

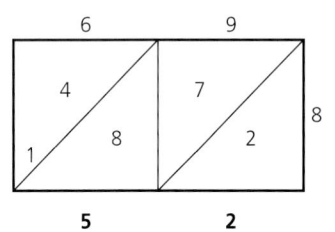

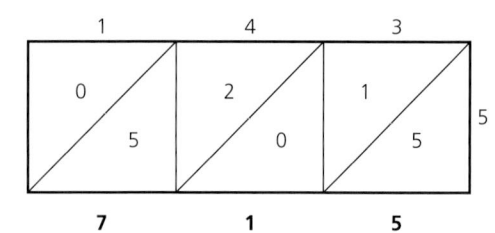

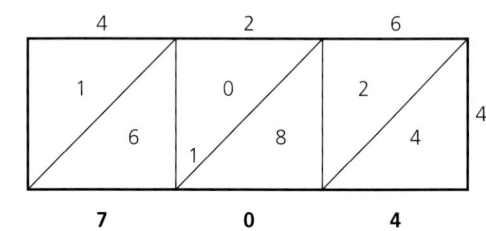

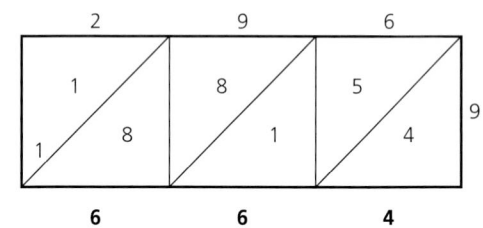

1 47 × 6 = 282

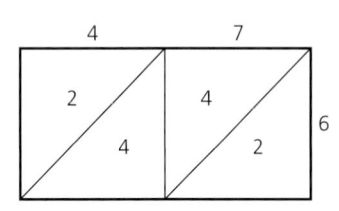

2 75 × 7 = 525

3 69 × 8 = 552

4 143 × 5 = 715

5 426 × 4 = 1704

6 296 × 9 = 2664

10 Division

This chapter follows the following elements of the National Curriculum for Year 4:

Number - Multiplication and division

Programme of study (statutory requirements)
Pupils should be taught to:
- recall multiplication and division facts for multiplication tables up to 12 × 12
- use place value, known and derived facts to multiply and divide mentally, including: multiplying by 0 and 1; dividing by 1; multiplying together 3 numbers

Notes and guidance (non-statutory)
- Pupils practise to become fluent in the formal written method of short multiplication for multiplying using multi-digit numbers, and short division with exact answers when dividing by a one-digit number.
- Pupils solve two-step problems in contexts, choosing the appropriate operation, working with increasingly harder numbers. This should include correspondence questions such as the numbers of choices of a meal on a menu, or three cakes shared equally between 10 children.

This chapter also covers the following elements not listed in the National Curriculum programme of study KS2:
- **Division with remainders**

■ Notes

■ Some practice with times tables and division would be useful before starting this chapter.

Exercise 10.1 Simple division

1. (a) 2   (c) 3   (e) 5   (g) 8   (i) 8
   (b) 3   (d) 3   (f) 10 (h) 5
2. (a) 4   (c) 8   (e) 4   (g) 7   (i) 12
   (b) 6   (d) 10 (f) 8   (h) 9
3. (a) 9   (c) 9   (e) 12
   (b) 11 (d) 12
4. (a) 2   (c) 5   (e) 7   (g) 7   (i) 5
   (b) 4   (d) 2   (f) 5   (h) 3   (j) 2

Exercise 10.2 Division with remainders

1. 5 r 4
2. 2 r 6
3. 9 r 2
4. 10 r 4
5. 11 r 1
6. 3 r 3
7. 2 r 8
8. 3 r 6
9. 2 r 6

Exercise 10.3 Dividing by 10, 100 and 1000

1. 8
2. 50
3. 42
4. 430
5. 868
6. 4
7. 19
8. 547
9. 400
10. 9000
11. 5
12. 96
13. 482
14. 320
15. 900
16. 8
17. 450
18. 610

Exercise 10.4 The formal method of division

1. 37
2. 28
3. 23
4. 13
5. 14
6. 13
7. 29
8. 14
9. 17
10. 54
11. 52
12. 34
13. 27
14. 23
15. 24
16. 15
17. 14
18. 32
19. 29
20. 23
21. 268
22. 247
23. 197
24. 115
25. 159
26. 123
27. 114
28. 198
29. 187
30. 287
31. 88
32. 52
33. 98
34. 63
35. 57
36. 75
37. 37
38. 47
39. 60
40. 208

Exercise 10.5 Checking answers

1. (a) $19 \times 4 = 76$ (b) $76 \div 4 = 19$
2. (a) $348 \div 6 = 58$ (b) $58 \times 6 = 348$
3. $5 \times 17 = 85$
4. $648 \div 3 = 216$
5. $7 \times 25 = 175$

6. ✓
7. ✗
8. ✓
9. ✓
10. ✗
11. ✓
12. ✗
13. ✓
14. ✓
15. ✗
16. ✗
17. ✓
18. ✓
19. ✓
20. ✗
21. ✗
22. ✓
23. ✗

Exercise 10.6 Problem solving

1. 6 mints
2. 14 boxes
3. 18 cherries
4. 3 taxis
5. 36 daffodils
6. 16 pencils
7. 50 boxes
8. 96 points
9. £225
10. 14 piles

Exercise 10.7 Problem solving with fractions

1 $\frac{1}{4}$ of a packet of biscuits

2 $\frac{1}{5}$ of a bag of sweets

3 $\frac{1}{12}$ of a cake

4 $\frac{3}{8}$ of a pizza

5 $\frac{3}{20}$ of a carton

6 $\frac{3}{16}$ of a bar of chocolate

7 $\frac{5}{10}$ or $\frac{1}{2}$ of a bar of chocolate

8 $\frac{2}{8}$ or $\frac{1}{4}$ of a pizza

9 $\frac{4}{16}$ or $\frac{1}{4}$ of a cake

10 $\frac{3}{9}$ or $\frac{1}{3}$ of a bar of chocolate

Exercise 10.8 Summary

1 (a) 7   (b) 5   (c) 9   (d) 10   (e) 5   (f) 7

2 (a) 12   (b) 160   (c) 4   (d) 35   (e) 800

3 (a) ✗   (b) ✓

4 (a) 14   (c) 13   (e) 64   (g) 139   (i) 102
   (b) 29   (d) 53   (f) 293   (h) 43

5 £55   6 $\frac{2}{5}$ of a bag   7 46 bunches   8 $\frac{3}{12}$ or $\frac{1}{4}$ of an orange

Activity – Pascal's triangle

								1							
							1		1						
						1		2		1					
					1		3		3		1				
				1		4		6		4		1			
			1		5		10		10		5		1		
		1		6		15		20		15		6		1	
	1		7		21		35		35		21		7		1
1		8		28		56		70		56		28		8		1
1	9		36		84		126		126		84		36		9		1
1	10	45		120		210		252		210		120		45	10	1

Patterns

- Each line starts and ends with 1
- Each number is the sum of the two numbers above it.
- The pattern is symmetrical about the centre.
- The total of each horizontal line is double the one above it.

11 Symmetry and reflection

This chapter follows the following elements of the National Curriculum for Year 4:

Geometry - Properties of shapes

Programme of study (statutory requirements)
Pupils should be taught to:
- identify lines of symmetry in 2D shapes presented in different orientations
- complete a simple symmetric figure with respect to a specific line of symmetry.

Notes and guidance (non-statutory)
- Pupils draw symmetric patterns using a variety of media to become familiar with different orientations of lines of symmetry; and recognise line symmetry in a variety of diagrams, including where the line of symmetry does not dissect the reflected shape.

■ Notes

■ Have available as many examples of symmetry as you can. The study of symmetry can be enriched by the use of dedicated maths software programs that enable pupils to explore reflection. Supported by this software, they can explore all the ideas in this chapter and beyond.

Exercise 11.1 Lines of symmetry and 2D shapes

1

Square
Right-angled isosceles triangle
Isosceles triangle
Isosceles trapezium
Rectangle

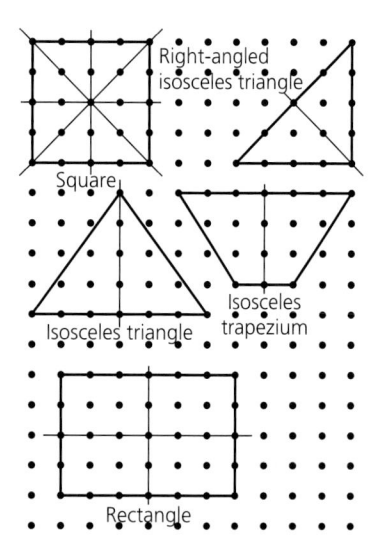

2

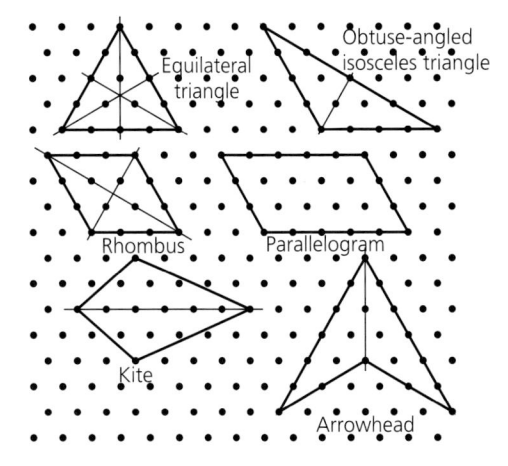

[Shapes on dot grid: Equilateral triangle, Obtuse-angled isosceles triangle, Rhombus, Parallelogram, Kite, Arrowhead — each with lines of symmetry drawn]

3

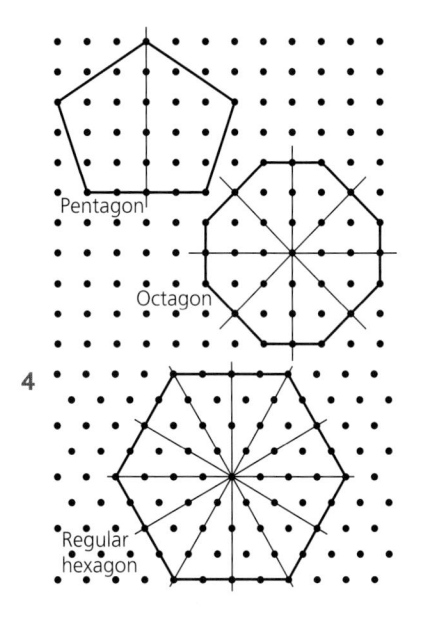

[Shapes on dot grid: Pentagon, Octagon — with lines of symmetry drawn]

4

[Regular hexagon on dot grid with lines of symmetry drawn]

5 (a)

	Name of shape	Number of sides	Number of lines of symmetry
(i)	Equilateral triangle	3	3
(ii)	Square	4	4
(iii)	Regular hexagon	6	6

(b) The sides are all equal.

(c) They are the same.

(d) 10; all 10 sides are equal and all 10 angles are equal.

Exercise 11.2 Symmetry and congruent shapes

1. (a) (i) EP   (ii) CQ
   (b) PA = PF or QB = QE
   (c) angle PEQ = x, angle BQC = y
   (d) They are congruent.

2. (a)

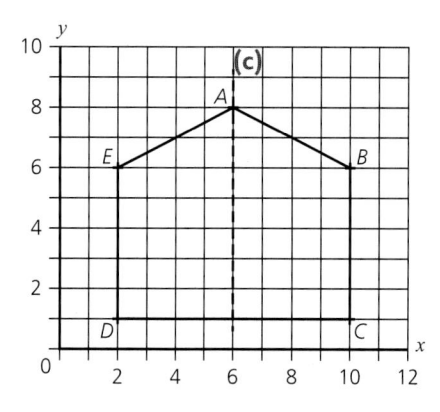

   (b) Pentagon
   (c) See grid
   (d) (i) AE   (ii) DE
   (e) Angle D
   (f) Triangle ADE

3. (a)

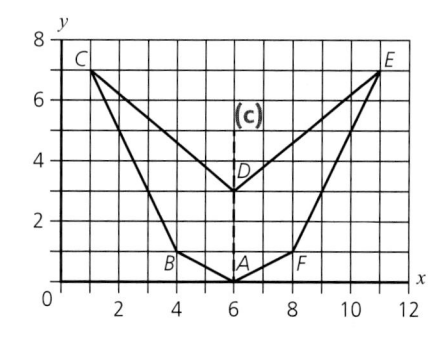

   (b) Hexagon
   (c) See grid
   (d) (i) AB   (ii) FE
   (e) Angle B
   (f) Triangle AFD

Exercise 11.3 Reflection

1. (a)   (b) 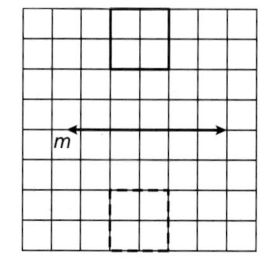   (c)

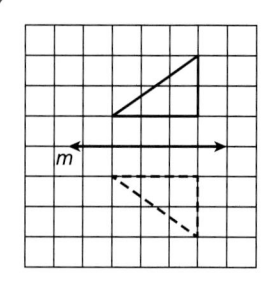

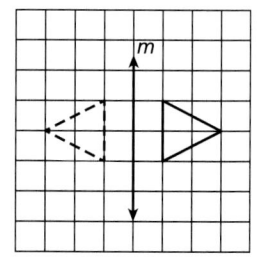

11 Symmetry and reflection

(d) (e) 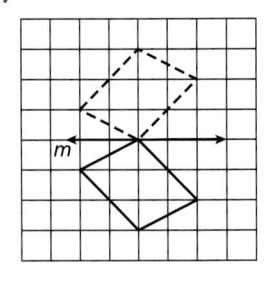 (f)

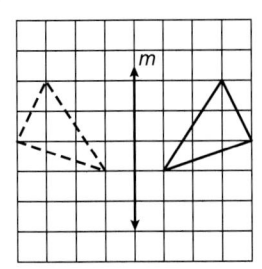

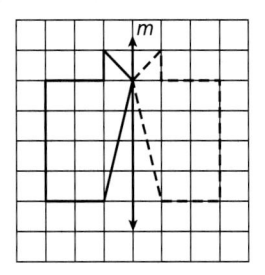

2 (a) 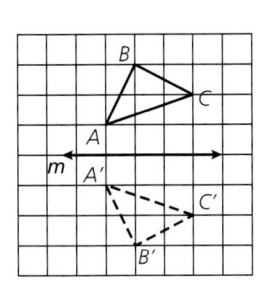 (c) 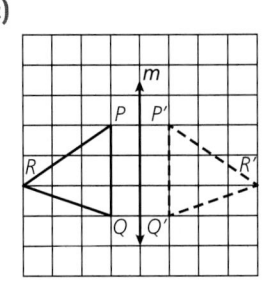 (e)

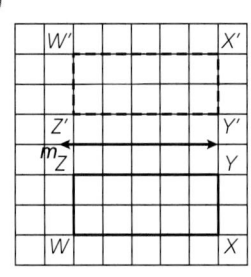

(b) 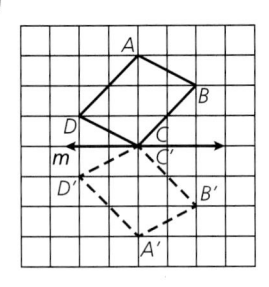 (d) 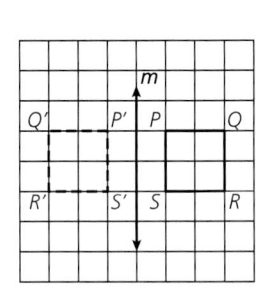 (f)

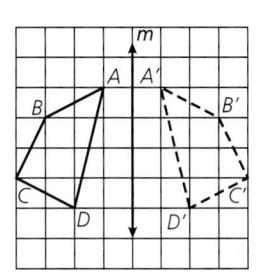

3 (a) 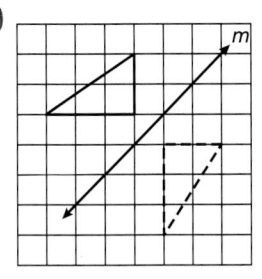 (b)

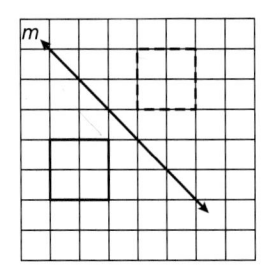

Activity – Symmetry in nature and design

Check pupils' designs

12 Mixed problems

This chapter follows the following elements of the National Curriculum for Year 4:

Number - Addition and subtraction

Programme of study (statutory requirements)
Pupils should be taught to:
- solve addition and subtraction two-step problems in contexts, deciding which operations and methods to use and why

Number - Multiplication and division

Programme of study (statutory requirements)
Pupils should be taught to:
- recall multiplication and division facts for multiplication tables up to 12 × 12
- use place value, known and derived facts to multiply and divide mentally, including: multiplying by 0 and 1; dividing by 1; multiplying together 3 numbers

Notes and guidance (non-statutory)
- Pupils solve two-step problems in contexts, choosing the appropriate operation, working with increasingly harder numbers. This should include correspondence questions such as the numbers of choices of a meal on a menu, or three cakes shared equally between 10 children.
- Pupils practise to become fluent in the formal written method of short multiplication for multiplying using multi-digit numbers, and short division with exact answers when dividing by a one-digit number.

Exercise 12.1 Multi-step problems

1. 40 bottles
2. 7 packs
3. 10 boxes
4. 9 loaves
5. 10 bags
6. 23 pupils
7. 47 music lessons
8. 145 house points
9. 1800 bricks
10. (a) 186 eggs
    (b) 15 egg boxes

Exercise 12.2 Formal calculations

1. (a) 54 pages   (b) 8 weeks
2. 23 seats
3. £230
4. 522 sheets
5. 600 pencils
6. 2664 books
7. £408
8. 16 journeys
9. 50 boxes
10. $22\frac{1}{2}$ strawberries

Activity – Missing digits (multiplication and division)

1.

	H	T	U
		2	3
×			4
		9	**2**

2.

	H	T	U
		2	7
×			3
		8	1

3.

	H	T	U
		5	6
×			7
	3	9	2

4.

	H	T	U
		6	1
×			9
	5	4	**9**

5.

	H	T	U
		6	9
×			7
	4	8	3

6.

	T	U
	3	2
3	9	**6**

7.

	H	T	U
		4	0
9	3	**6**	0

8.

	H	T	U
		5	1
8	4	0	8

9.

	H	T	U
		4	**3**
3	1	**2**	9

10.

	H	T	U
	1	9	7
5	**9**	8	**5**

12 Mixed problems

43

13 Sequences

This chapter follows the following elements of the National Curriculum for Year 4:

Number - Addition and subtraction

Programme of study (statutory requirements)
Pupils should be taught to:
- solve addition and subtraction two-step problems in contexts, deciding which operations and methods to use and why

Number - Multiplication and division

Programme of study (statutory requirements)
Pupils should be taught to:
- recall multiplication and division facts for multiplication tables up to 12 × 12

Notes and guidance (non-statutory)
- Pupils solve two-step problems in contexts, choosing the appropriate operation, working with increasingly harder numbers. This should include correspondence questions such as the numbers of choices of a meal on a menu, or three cakes shared equally between 10 children.

This chapter also covers the following elements not listed in the National Curriculum programme of study KS2:
- Sequences

■ Notes

■ You may need to review negative numbers before starting this chapter.

Exercise 13.1 Simple sequences

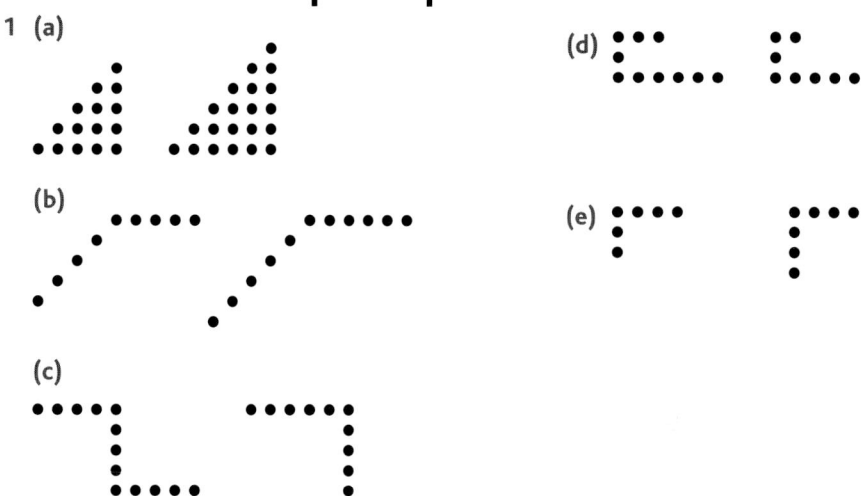

1 (a), (b), (c), (d), (e)

2 (a) (i) add 2
       (ii) 21   23
   (b) (i) add 7
       (ii) 42   49
   (c) (i) divide by 10
       (ii) 10   1
   (d) (i) add 2
       (ii) 3   5
   (e) (i) subtract 2
       (ii) 0   ⁻2
   (f) (i) add 3
       (ii) 0   3
   (g) (i) divide by 2
       (ii) 2   1
   (h) (i) subtract 1, subtract 2, subtract 3 ...
       (ii) 10   5
   (i) (i) square numbers
       (ii) 25   36
   (j) (i) add previous two terms together
       (ii) 13   21

3 (a) 12   (e) 46   (i) 5   (m) 1   17
   (b) 6   (f) 4   (j) 50   (n) 26   21
   (c) 21   (g) 14   (k) 150   (o) ⁻2   10
   (d) 19   (h) ⁻2   (l) 9   3   (p) 14

Exercise 13.2 Writing a sequence from a rule

1	3	5	7	9	11	1	3	5	7
2	2	4	8	16	12	6	10	14	18
3	24	20	16	12	13	3	5	11	29
4	8	4	2	1	14	1	2	4	8
5	3	6	12	24	15	2	6	14	30
6	6	3	0	⁻3	16	2	8	20	44
7	⁻5	⁻2	1	4	17	5	9	17	33
8	7	70	700	7000	18	5	8	14	26
9	49	38	27	16	19	1	6	21	66
10	25	50	75	100	20	1	1	1	1

14 Time

This chapter follows the following elements of the National Curriculum for Year 4:

Measurement - Time

Programme of study (statutory requirements)
Pupils should be taught to:
- convert between different units of measure (for example, kilometre to metre; hour to minute)
- read, write and convert time between analogue and digital 12 and 24-hour clocks
- solve problems involving converting from hours to minutes; minutes to seconds; years to months; weeks to days

This chapter also covers the following elements not listed in the National Curriculum programme of study KS2:
- The calendar

■ Notes

■ Pupils may be lacking in confidence in this area and therefore it is revised in this chapter.

Exercise 14.1 The analogue clock

1. (a) 9 o'clock
   (b) half past 1
   (c) quarter past 9
   (d) quarter to 9

2. (a) twenty past 2
   (b) twenty to 8
   (c) ten past 5

3. (a) five past 8
   (b) twenty-five to 4
   (c) five to 3

4. (a) seven minutes past 4
   (b) seventeen minutes to 12
   (c) twenty-eight minutes past 3

5. (a) (b)  (c)  (d)

46

6 (a)   (b)    (c) 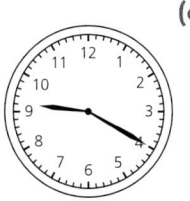   (d)

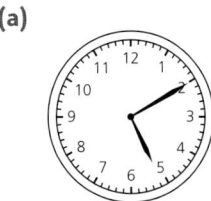

7 (a)    (b)    (c)    (d)

8 (a)    (b)    (c)    (d)

Exercise 14.2 The digital clock

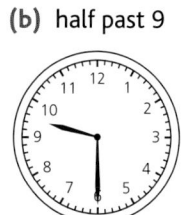

1 (a) twenty-five past 2   (c) ten to 3
  (b) half past 6   (d) 22 minutes to 11

2 (a) quarter past 11   (d) eight minutes to 6
  (b) quarter to 5   (e) eight minutes past 6
  (c) twenty-five past 8   (f) nineteen minutes past 12

3 (a) quarter past 1   (c) twenty-five to 8   (e) twelve minutes past 4

  (b) half past 9   (d) five to 12   (f) eighteen minutes to 3

4 (a) 3:45   (c) 7:30   (e) 1:55
   (b) 10:15   (d) 6:10   (f) 4:35

Exercise 14.3 The 24-hour clock

1 (a) 06:00   (c) 11:20   (e) 23:50
   (b) 19:00   (d) 15:45   (f) 19:05

2 (a) 8.30 a.m.   (c) 10.15 a.m.   (e) 7.45 p.m.
   (b) 10.05 p.m.   (d) 4.20 p.m.   (f) 12.35 p.m.

3 (a) 09:43   (c) 04:06   (e) 00:15
   (b) 23:32   (d) 19:54   (f) 12:36

4 (a) 11.12 a.m.   (c) 12.46 p.m.   (e) 9.23 a.m.
   (b) 8.43 p.m.   (d) 4.12 p.m.   (f) 12.12 a.m.

5 Question 3:
   (a) seventeen minutes to 10   (d) six minutes to 8
   (b) twenty-eight minutes to 12   (e) quarter past midnight
   (c) six minutes past 4   (f) twenty-four minutes to 1

   Question 4:
   (a) twelve minutes past 11   (d) twelve minutes past 4
   (b) seventeen minutes to 9   (e) twenty-three minutes past 9
   (c) fourteen minutes to 1   (f) twelve minutes past midnight

6 Question 3:

Question 4:

(a) (c)  (e)

(b)  (d)  (f)

Exercise 14.4 More units of time

1. (a) 120 seconds (c) 600 seconds
   (b) 300 seconds (d) 1800 seconds
2. (a) 3 minutes (c) 6 minutes
   (b) 4 minutes (d) $\frac{1}{2}$ minute
3. (a) 75 seconds (c) 445 seconds
   (b) 150 seconds (d) 252 seconds
4. (a) 1 minute 40 seconds (c) 3 minutes 25 seconds
   (b) 2 minutes 10 seconds (d) 6 minutes 40 seconds
5. (a) 1 week 3 days (c) 4 weeks 2 days
   (b) 2 weeks 6 days (d) 5 weeks 5 days
6. (a) 14 days (b) 28 days (c) 25 days (d) 75 days
7. (a) 92 days (b) 92 days (c) 123 days
8. (a) 2016 and (c) 2020
9. 2020–2029 (3, 2030–2039 will have 2)
10. (a) 48 months (b) 72 months (c) 240 months

Exercise 14.5 Problem solving

1. 2012, 2016, 2020, 2024, 2028
2. 49 days
3. 72 hours
4. 5 hours 20 minutes
5. 91 minutes *or* 1 hour 31 minutes
6. 50 days
7. (a) 146 minutes
   (b) 8812 seconds
8. 122 days old
9. (a) 2 hours 40 minutes
   (b) 26 hours 40 minutes
10. (a) 37 weeks and 1 day
    (b) 8 months, 2 weeks and 6 days

Exercise 14.6 Summary

1. (a) (i) quarter past 6
      (ii) 18:15
   (b) (i) ten to 3
      (ii) 14:50
   (c) (i) seventeen minutes past 9
      (ii) 21:17
   (d) (i) twenty-three minutes past 12
      (ii) 12:23
   (e) (i) eighteen minutes to 7
      (ii) 18:42
   (f) (i) four minutes past 4
      (ii) 16:04

2. (a) (ii) 07:45
   (b) (ii) 03:30
   (c) (ii) 10:55
   (d) (ii) 09:26
   (e) (ii) 01:48
   (f) (ii) 00:09

3. (a) 08:45
   (b) 23:45
   (c) 15:45
   (d) 23:12
   (e) 00:06
   (f) 18:55

4 (a) (i) 5.00 p.m.
        (ii) five o'clock
   (b) (i) 9.30 a.m.
        (ii) half past 9
   (c) (i) 1.15 p.m.
        (ii) quarter past 1
   (d) (i) 8.34 a.m.
        (ii) twenty-six minutes to 9
   (e) (i) 11.16 p.m.
        (ii) Sixteen minutes past 11
   (f) (i) 12.25 a.m.
        (ii) twenty-five minutes past midnight

5 (a) 5 weeks 3 days
   (b) 1 minute 35 seconds
   (c) 360 seconds
   (d) 41 months
   (e) 912 minutes
   (f) 2 years 6 months

6 91 days

7 140 minutes *or* 2 hours 20 minutes

8 (a) 192 minutes   (b) 11 530 seconds

9 190 minutes *or* 3 hours 10 minutes

10 (a) 6 minutes and 30 seconds   (b) 390 seconds

Activity – The calendar

The game will help pupils develop their vocabulary and understanding of the calendar.

Pupils' answers will depend on the year on the calendar.

This is neat investigation for Year 4 as they can investigate systematically, draw a conclusion and explain why it is correct.

They should discover that:

- for months with 31 days, the end day is 2 days after the start day
- for months with 30 days, the end day is 1 day after the start day

This is because 31 ÷ 7 = 4 r 3 and 30 ÷ 7 = 4 r 2 but you must take away 1 from the remainder.

Do encourage lots of chat!

You could also cut months of a calendar into strips or jigsaw pieces and have them piece it together again.

You can use the numbers from old calendars as a useful source of digit cards for various games.

15 Fractions

This chapter follows the following elements of the National Curriculum for Year 4:

Number - Number and place value

Notes and guidance (non-statutory)
- Pupils should connect hundredths to tenths and place value and decimal measure.

Number - Fractions
Programme of study (statutory requirements)
Pupils should be taught to:
- recognise and show, using diagrams, families of common equivalent fractions
- add and subtract fractions with the same denominator

Notes and guidance (non-statutory)
- They extend the use of the number line to connect fractions, numbers and measures.
- They practise counting using simple fractions and decimal fractions, both forwards and backwards.
- Pupils make connections between fractions of a length, of a shape and as a representation of one whole or set of quantities. Pupils use factors and multiples to recognise equivalent fractions and simplify where appropriate (e.g. $\frac{6}{9} = \frac{2}{3}$ or $\frac{1}{4} = \frac{2}{8}$)
- Pupils continue to practice adding and subtracting fractions with the same denominator, to become fluent through a variety of increasingly complex problems beyond one whole.

■ Notes

- The National Curriculum includes counting forwards and backwards in fractions and in decimal fractions. This is covered in the first two exercises, but it is also a useful warm-up activity for any lesson.
- The initial work on number lines can be revisited once pupils have revised equivalent fractions.

Exercise 15.1 Fractions on the number line
Check pupils' number lines

Exercise 15.2 Counting in fractions
Oral work

Exercise 15.3 Equivalent fractions
Rectangles may be coloured differently.

1 $\frac{1}{4} = \frac{2}{8}$

2 $\frac{1}{2} = \frac{3}{6}$

3 $\frac{1}{5} = \frac{2}{10}$

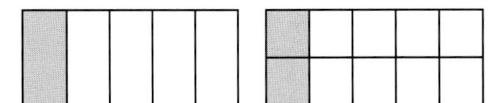

4 $\frac{2}{5} = \frac{4}{10}$

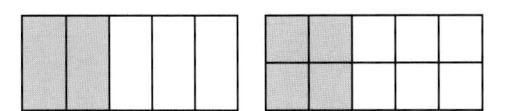

5 $\frac{3}{5} = \frac{6}{10}$

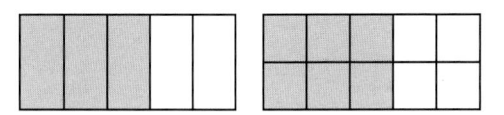

6 $\frac{1}{3} = \frac{2}{6}$

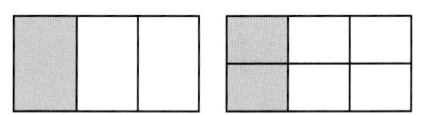

7 $\frac{2}{3} = \frac{4}{6}$

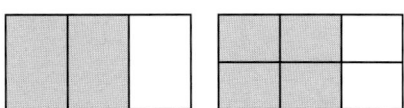

8 $\frac{2}{3} = \frac{6}{9}$

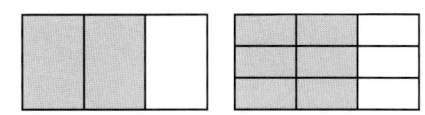

9 $\frac{3}{8} = \frac{9}{24}$

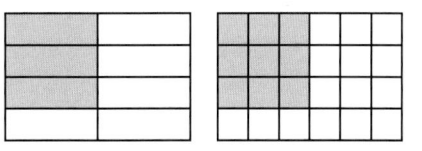

10 $\frac{5}{12} = \frac{10}{24}$

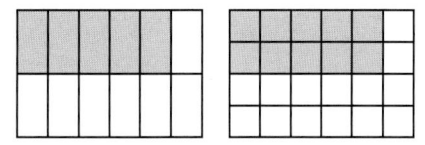

11

sixths	$\frac{1}{6}$	$\frac{2}{6}$	$\frac{3}{6}$	$\frac{4}{6}$	$\frac{5}{6}$
thirds		$\frac{1}{3}$		$\frac{2}{3}$	
halves			$\frac{1}{2}$		

12

eighths	$\frac{1}{8}$	$\frac{2}{8}$	$\frac{3}{8}$	$\frac{4}{8}$	$\frac{5}{8}$	$\frac{6}{8}$	$\frac{7}{8}$
quarters		$\frac{1}{4}$				$\frac{3}{4}$	
halves				$\frac{1}{2}$			

13

tenths	$\frac{1}{10}$	$\frac{2}{10}$	$\frac{3}{10}$	$\frac{4}{10}$	$\frac{5}{10}$	$\frac{6}{10}$	$\frac{7}{10}$	$\frac{8}{10}$	$\frac{9}{10}$
fifths and halves		$\frac{1}{5}$		$\frac{2}{5}$	$\frac{1}{2}$	$\frac{3}{5}$		$\frac{4}{5}$	

14

twelfths	$\frac{1}{12}$	$\frac{2}{12}$	$\frac{3}{12}$	$\frac{4}{12}$	$\frac{5}{12}$	$\frac{6}{12}$	$\frac{7}{12}$	$\frac{8}{12}$	$\frac{9}{12}$	$\frac{10}{12}$	$\frac{11}{12}$
equivalent fractions		$\frac{1}{6}$	$\frac{1}{4}$	$\frac{1}{3}$		$\frac{1}{2}$		$\frac{2}{3}$	$\frac{3}{4}$	$\frac{5}{6}$	

Exercise 15.4 Calculating equivalent fractions

1. $\frac{1}{2} = \frac{5}{10}$
2. $\frac{1}{4} = \frac{3}{12}$
3. $\frac{6}{12} = \frac{1}{2}$
4. $\frac{9}{12} = \frac{3}{4}$
5. $\frac{1}{2} = \frac{4}{8}$
6. $\frac{2}{3} = \frac{8}{12}$
7. $\frac{10}{12} = \frac{5}{6}$
8. $\frac{5}{6} = \frac{10}{12}$
9. $\frac{5}{15} = \frac{1}{3}$
10. $\frac{10}{15} = \frac{2}{3}$
11. $\frac{2}{3} = \frac{10}{15}$
12. $\frac{4}{5} = \frac{12}{15}$
13. $\frac{3}{10} = \frac{6}{20}$
14. $\frac{2}{5} = \frac{10}{25}$
15. $\frac{15}{50} = \frac{3}{10}$
16. $\frac{5}{8} = \frac{25}{40}$
17. $\frac{12}{30} = \frac{4}{10}$
18. $\frac{3}{5} = \frac{15}{25}$
19. $\frac{3}{4} = \frac{18}{24}$
20. $\frac{7}{10} = \frac{28}{40}$

Exercise 15.5 Simplest form

1. (a) $\frac{6}{24} = \frac{1}{4}$
   (b) $\frac{8}{24} = \frac{1}{3}$
   (c) $\frac{3}{15} = \frac{1}{5}$
   (d) $\frac{4}{10} = \frac{2}{5}$
   (e) $\frac{6}{18} = \frac{1}{3}$
   (f) $\frac{12}{18} = \frac{2}{3}$
   (g) $\frac{9}{18} = \frac{1}{2}$
   (h) $\frac{15}{24} = \frac{5}{8}$
   (i) $\frac{18}{24} = \frac{3}{4}$

2. (a) $\frac{4}{5}$
   (b) $\frac{2}{3}$
   (c) $\frac{1}{2}$
   (d) $\frac{1}{3}$
   (e) $\frac{3}{4}$
   (f) $\frac{3}{4}$
   (g) $\frac{2}{3}$
   (h) $\frac{2}{3}$
   (i) $\frac{3}{8}$
   (j) $\frac{2}{3}$
   (k) $\frac{3}{5}$
   (l) $\frac{3}{5}$
   (m) $\frac{3}{5}$
   (n) $\frac{3}{4}$
   (o) $\frac{1}{2}$
   (p) $\frac{5}{6}$
   (q) $\frac{2}{5}$
   (r) $\frac{3}{4}$
   (s) $\frac{18}{25}$
   (t) $\frac{11}{20}$

Exercise 15.6 Writing fractions

1. $\frac{1}{2}$

2. (a) $\frac{1}{3}$ (b) $\frac{2}{3}$

3. (a) $\frac{4}{9}$ (b) $\frac{5}{9}$

4. (a) $\frac{2}{3}$ (b) $\frac{1}{3}$

5 (a) (i) $\frac{1}{2}$ (c) (i) $\frac{1}{3}$ (e) (i) $\frac{2}{3}$ (g) (i) $\frac{1}{6}$

     (ii) $\frac{1}{2}$ (ii) $\frac{2}{3}$ (ii) $\frac{1}{3}$ (ii) $\frac{5}{6}$

   (b) (i) $\frac{1}{4}$ (d) (i) $\frac{2}{5}$ (f) (i) $\frac{1}{3}$ (h) (i) $\frac{1}{2}$

     (ii) $\frac{3}{4}$ (ii) $\frac{3}{5}$ (ii) $\frac{2}{3}$ (ii) $\frac{1}{2}$

6 (a) $\frac{2}{9}$ (b) $\frac{1}{3}$ (c) $\frac{4}{9}$

7 (a) $\frac{3}{5}$ (b) $\frac{2}{5}$

8 (a) $\frac{4}{5}$ (b) $\frac{1}{5}$

9 (a) $\frac{11}{16}$ (b) $\frac{5}{16}$

10 (a) $\frac{4}{9}$ (b) $\frac{1}{3}$ (c) $\frac{2}{9}$

11 (a) $\frac{1}{4}$ (b) $\frac{1}{3}$ (c) $\frac{5}{12}$

Exercise 15.7 Fractions greater than 1

1 (a) 1   (c) 5   (e) 2   (g) 6   (i) 4

   (b) 1   (d) 3   (f) 3   (h) 3   (j) 3

2 (a) $1\frac{1}{6}$ (f) $2\frac{1}{3}$ (k) $3\frac{1}{6}$ (p) $7\frac{2}{3}$

   (b) $1\frac{3}{7}$ (g) $2\frac{3}{5}$ (l) $3\frac{3}{10}$ (q) $6\frac{3}{4}$

   (c) $1\frac{3}{8}$ (h) $2\frac{3}{4}$ (m) $2\frac{5}{8}$ (r) $6\frac{5}{6}$

   (d) $1\frac{1}{5}$ (i) $2\frac{3}{7}$ (n) $4\frac{4}{5}$ (s) $4\frac{3}{8}$

   (e) $1\frac{4}{5}$ (j) $2\frac{2}{9}$ (o) $6\frac{1}{2}$ (t) $4\frac{9}{10}$

3 (a) $1\frac{1}{2}$ (e) $2\frac{3}{5}$ (i) $1\frac{1}{2}$ (m) $1\frac{1}{2}$

   (b) $1\frac{1}{3}$ (f) $1\frac{1}{4}$ (j) $1\frac{3}{4}$ (n) $1\frac{2}{5}$

   (c) $2\frac{1}{2}$ (g) $1\frac{1}{5}$ (k) $1\frac{2}{7}$ (o) $1\frac{1}{4}$

   (d) $2\frac{2}{3}$ (h) $1\frac{1}{5}$ (l) $1\frac{3}{8}$ (p) $3\frac{1}{5}$

Exercise 15.8 Fractions and division

1. $1\frac{5}{7}$
2. $2\frac{4}{5}$
3. $2\frac{1}{8}$
4. $5\frac{5}{6}$
5. $3\frac{4}{5}$
6. $3\frac{2}{9}$
7. $4\frac{3}{4}$
8. $4\frac{1}{6}$
9. $3\frac{7}{10}$

Exercise 15.9 Writing mixed numbers as improper fractions

1. $\frac{3}{2}$
2. $\frac{7}{4}$
3. $\frac{17}{10}$
4. $\frac{11}{6}$
5. $\frac{8}{3}$
6. $\frac{13}{5}$
7. $\frac{31}{12}$
8. $\frac{41}{15}$
9. $\frac{19}{5}$
10. $\frac{34}{9}$
11. $\frac{39}{10}$
12. $\frac{14}{3}$
13. $\frac{32}{7}$
14. $\frac{43}{10}$
15. $\frac{52}{11}$
16. $\frac{17}{3}$
17. $\frac{41}{7}$
18. $\frac{53}{9}$
19. $\frac{49}{8}$
20. $\frac{15}{2}$
21. $\frac{25}{6}$
22. $\frac{25}{3}$
23. $\frac{39}{20}$
24. $\frac{43}{15}$
25. $\frac{57}{25}$
26. $\frac{41}{12}$
27. $\frac{44}{9}$
28. $\frac{27}{4}$
29. $\frac{22}{3}$
30. $\frac{53}{5}$
31. $\frac{71}{8}$
32. $\frac{65}{7}$

Exercise 15.10 Summary

1. *The rectangles may be coloured differently.*

    (a) $\frac{1}{3} = \frac{3}{9}$
    (b) $\frac{5}{8} = \frac{15}{24}$

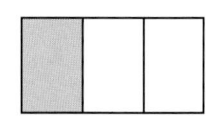

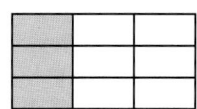

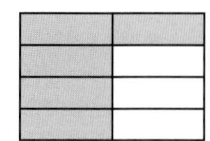

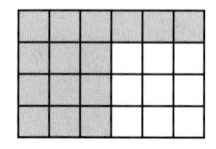

2. (a) $\frac{1}{2} = \frac{4}{8}$
   (b) $\frac{1}{4} = \frac{4}{16}$
   (c) $\frac{8}{12} = \frac{2}{3}$
   (d) $\frac{9}{15} = \frac{3}{5}$

3. (a) $\frac{1}{5}$
   (b) $\frac{4}{5}$

4. (a) (i) $\frac{1}{2}$ (ii) $\frac{1}{2}$ (b) (i) $\frac{5}{12}$ (ii) $\frac{7}{12}$

5 (a) $\dfrac{1}{5}$ (b) $\dfrac{1}{3}$ (c) $\dfrac{7}{15}$

6 (a) $1\dfrac{1}{3}$ (b) $1\dfrac{3}{5}$ (c) $2\dfrac{1}{4}$ (d) $1\dfrac{7}{10}$

7 (a) $\dfrac{3}{2}$ (b) $\dfrac{10}{3}$ (c) $\dfrac{39}{4}$ (d) $\dfrac{25}{7}$

Activity – Equivalent squares

The instructions provide a simple progression through this activity.

One solution is shown below.

16 Calculating with fractions

This chapter follows the following elements of the National Curriculum for Year 4:

Number - Fractions
Programme of study (statutory requirements)
Pupils should be taught to:
- recognise and show, using diagrams, families of common equivalent fractions
- add and subtract fractions with the same denominator

Notes and guidance (non-statutory)
- Pupils use factors and multiples to recognise equivalent fractions and simplify where appropriate (e.g. $\frac{6}{9} = \frac{2}{3}$ or $\frac{1}{4} = \frac{2}{8}$)
- Pupils continue to practice adding and subtracting fractions with the same denominator, to become fluent through a variety of increasingly complex problems beyond one whole.

■ Notes

- There are more calculations with fractions in later chapters.
- Give pupils fraction circles if they need concrete aids for support.

Exercise 16.1 Adding fractions

1. $\frac{3}{5}$
2. 1
3. 1
4. $\frac{1}{2}$
5. $1\frac{1}{5}$
6. $1\frac{1}{3}$
7. $1\frac{2}{9}$
8. $1\frac{3}{5}$
9. $1\frac{2}{7}$
10. $1\frac{2}{11}$
11. $\frac{2}{3}$
12. $\frac{1}{2}$
13. $1\frac{5}{6}$
14. 2
15. $1\frac{7}{8}$
16. 2
17. $1\frac{2}{3}$
18. 2

Exercise 16.2 Subtracting fractions

As with any subtractions, encourage pupils to check their answers by addition.

1. $\frac{3}{5}$
2. $\frac{1}{2}$
3. $\frac{3}{4}$
4. $\frac{5}{9}$
5. $\frac{2}{5}$
6. $\frac{4}{5}$
7. $\frac{1}{6}$
8. $\frac{4}{5}$
9. $\frac{1}{2}$
10. $1\frac{1}{5}$
11. $1\frac{1}{2}$
12. $1\frac{2}{3}$
13. $1\frac{1}{3}$
14. $1\frac{4}{11}$
15. $1\frac{3}{5}$
16. $1\frac{1}{6}$
17. $1\frac{3}{5}$
18. $1\frac{2}{5}$

Exercise 16.3 Using improper fractions to subtract

1. $\frac{2}{3}$
2. $\frac{1}{2}$
3. $\frac{2}{3}$
4. $\frac{4}{5}$
5. $\frac{1}{2}$
6. $\frac{3}{5}$
7. $\frac{5}{7}$
8. $\frac{2}{3}$
9. $\frac{1}{2}$
10. $\frac{2}{3}$

Exercise 16.4 Missing numbers

1. $\frac{3}{5} + \frac{2}{5} = 1$
2. $\frac{7}{8} - \frac{3}{8} = \frac{1}{2}$
3. $\frac{7}{8} - \frac{1}{8} = \frac{3}{4}$
4. $\frac{7}{9} - \frac{4}{9} = \frac{1}{3}$
5. $\frac{7}{9} - \frac{1}{9} = \frac{2}{3}$
6. $\frac{4}{10} + \frac{1}{10} = \frac{1}{2} \left(or\ \frac{2}{5} \right)$
7. $\frac{7}{10} - \frac{3}{10} = \frac{2}{5}$
8. $\frac{1}{12} + \frac{2}{12} = \frac{1}{4} \left(or\ \frac{1}{6} \right)$
9. $\frac{12}{15} - \frac{9}{15} = \frac{1}{5} \left(or\ \frac{4}{5} \right)$
10. $\frac{3}{10} + \frac{5}{10} = \frac{4}{5} \left(or\ \frac{1}{2} \right)$
11. $\frac{2}{5} + \frac{4}{5} = 1\frac{1}{5}$
12. $1\frac{3}{4} - 1\frac{1}{4} = \frac{1}{2}$
13. $1\frac{4}{10} + \frac{1}{10} = 1\frac{1}{2} \left(or\ \frac{2}{5} \right)$
14. $1\frac{3}{10} - \frac{8}{10} = \frac{1}{2} \left(or\ \frac{4}{5} \right)$
15. $1\frac{2}{12} - \frac{5}{12} = \frac{3}{4} \left(or\ \frac{1}{6} \right)$
16. $1\frac{1}{8} + \frac{3}{8} = 1\frac{1}{2}$
17. $1\frac{7}{15} - \frac{12}{15} = \frac{2}{3} \left(or\ \frac{4}{5} \right)$
18. $1\frac{1}{12} + \frac{8}{12} = 1\frac{3}{4} \left(or\ \frac{2}{3}\ or\ \frac{4}{6} \right)$

Exercise 16.5 Summary

1. (a) $\frac{4}{5}$ (b) $1\frac{1}{5}$ (c) $1\frac{1}{4}$ (d) $1\frac{3}{5}$ (e) $1\frac{3}{5}$ (f) $1\frac{11}{12}$

2. (a) $\frac{3}{5}$ (b) $\frac{1}{4}$ (c) $\frac{5}{6}$ (d) $1\frac{1}{3}$ (e) $\frac{1}{2}$ (f) $\frac{1}{2}$

3. (a) $\frac{1}{8} + \frac{5}{8} = 1$ (d) $\frac{4}{5} - \frac{1}{5} = \frac{3}{5}$

   (b) $\frac{7}{10} - \frac{3}{10} = \frac{4}{10}$ (e) $1\frac{5}{12} + \frac{4}{12} = 1\frac{3}{4} \left(or\ \frac{1}{3}\ or\ \frac{2}{6} \right)$

   (c) $\frac{1}{12} + \frac{1}{6} = \frac{1}{4} \left(or\ \frac{2}{12} \right)$ (f) $1\frac{1}{8} - \frac{5}{8} = \frac{1}{2}$

Activity – Four and twenty

The answers given will depend on pupils' prior knowledge, for example, whether they know that $\sqrt{4} = 2$

Possible answers:

$0 = 4 - 4$

$1 = 4 \div 4$

$2 = \frac{4}{4} + \frac{4}{4}$

$3 = 4 - \frac{4}{4}$

$4 = 4$

$5 = 4 + \frac{4}{4}$

$6 = 4 + \frac{4}{4} + \frac{4}{4}$

$7 = 4 + 4 - \frac{4}{4}$

$8 = 4 + 4$

$9 = 4 + 4 + \frac{4}{4}$

$10 = \frac{44}{4} - \frac{4}{4}$

$11 = \frac{44}{4}$

$12 = 4 + 4 + 4$

$13 = 4 + 4 + 4 + \frac{4}{4}$

$14 = 4 \times 4 - \frac{4}{4} - \frac{4}{4}$

$15 = \frac{44}{4} + 4$

$16 = 4 \times 4$

$17 = 4 \times 4 + \frac{4}{4}$

$18 = 4 \times 4 + \frac{4}{4} + \frac{4}{4}$

$19 = 4 \times 4 + 4 - \frac{4}{4}$

$20 = 4 \times \left(4 + \frac{4}{4}\right)$

17 Fractions and decimals

This chapter follows the following elements of the National Curriculum for Year 4:

Number - Number and place value

Notes and guidance (non-statutory)
- Pupils should connect hundredths to tenths and place value and decimal measure.

Number - Fractions (including decimals)

Programme of study (statutory requirements)
Pupils should be taught to:
- find the effect of dividing a one- or two-digit number by 10 and 100, identifying the value of the digits in the answer as units, tenths and hundredths
- count up and down in hundredths; recognise that hundredths arise when dividing an object by a hundred and dividing tenths by ten
- compare numbers with the same number of decimal places up to two decimal places
- recognise and write decimal equivalents of any number of tenths or hundredths
- recognise and write decimal equivalents to $\frac{1}{4}$; $\frac{1}{2}$; $\frac{3}{4}$
- round decimals with one decimal place to the nearest whole number

Notes and guidance (non-statutory)
- They begin to extend their knowledge of the number system to include the decimal numbers and fractions that they have met so far.
- Pupils are taught throughout that decimals and fractions are different ways of expressing numbers and proportions.
- They practise counting using simple fractions and decimal fractions, both forwards and backwards. Pupils learn decimal notation and the language associated with it.
- They should be able to represent numbers with one or two decimal places in several ways, such as on number lines.

■ Notes

- This chapter builds on the previous work on fractions.
- Pupils who find the concept difficult can use number lines for support. You may wish to do Chapter 21 Money before you do this.
- Counting on and back in tenths and hundredths is a good warm-up activity.
- It is really important that pupils understand the basic concept as it is vital in measurement. The later practical examples in the chapters on money, measurement and reading scales will help to reinforce this work.

Exercise 17.1 Place value

1. $\frac{3}{10}$
2. $\frac{7}{100}$
3. $\frac{7}{1000}$
4. $\frac{3}{100}$
5. $\frac{1}{1000}$
6. $\frac{7}{10}$
7. $\frac{9}{1000}$
8. $\frac{9}{10}$

9   $\frac{9}{100}$
10 $\frac{7}{10}$
11 $\frac{9}{100}$
12 $\frac{7}{1000}$
13 $\frac{3}{10}$
14 6
15 $\frac{3}{100}$
16 $\frac{7}{1000}$
17 20
18 $\frac{1}{10}$
19 200
20 $\frac{3}{100}$
21 $\frac{3}{10}$
22 80
23 4000
24 $\frac{7}{1000}$
25 2

Exercise 17.2 Counting in tenths

1 (a) 0, 0.1, 0.2, 0.3, 0.4, 0.5, 0.6, 0.7, 0.8

(b) 0.7, 0.8, 0.9, 1.0, 1.1, 1.2, 1.3, 1.4, 1.5

(c) 2, 2.1, 2.2, 2.3, 2.4, 2.5, 2.6, 2.7, 2.8, 2.9, 3

(d) 4.5, 4.6, 4.7, 4.8, 4.9, 5.0, 5.1, 5.2, 5.3, 5.4, 5.5

2 (a) 0.1   0.2   0.3   0.4   0.5   0.6   0.7

(b) 0.5   0.6   0.7   0.8   0.9   1.0   1.1

(c) 1.4   1.5   1.6   1.7   1.8   1.9   2

(d) 1.8   1.9   2.0   2.1   2.2   2.3   2.4

(e) 12.6 12.7 12.8 12.9 13.0 13.1 13.2

(f) 25.8 25.9 26.0 26.1 26.2 26.3 26.4

3 (a) 0.7   (c) 2.0   (e) 3.1

(b) 1.1   (d) 2.2   (f) 26.5

4 (a) 0.9   0.8   0.7   0.6   0.5   0.4   0.3

(b) 1.8   1.7   1.6   1.5   1.4   1.3   1.2

(c) 1.2   1.1   1.0   0.9   0.8   0.7   0.6

(d) 2.8   2.7   2.6   2.5   2.4   2.3   2.2

(e) 12.3 12.2 12.1 12.0 11.9 11.8 11.7

(f) 27.1 27.0 26.9 26.8 26.7 26.6 26.5

5 (a) 0.3   (c) 0.6   (e) 11.7

(b) 1.2   (d) 1.9   (f) 24.5

Exercise 17.3 Counting in hundredths

1 (a) 0, 0.01, 0.02, 0.03, 0.04, 0.05, 0.06, 0.07

(b) 0.05, 0.06, 0.07, 0.08, 0.09, 0.10, 0.11, 0.12, 0.13, 0.14

(c) 1.15, 1.16, 1.17, 1.18, 1.19, 1.20, 1.21, 1.22, 1.23, 1.24, 1.25

(d) 3.95, 3.96, 3.97, 3.98, 3.99, 4.00, 4.01, 4.02, 4.03, 4.04, 4.05

2 (a) 0.01 0.02 0.03 0.04 0.05 0.06 0.07

(b) 0.05 0.06 0.07 0.08 0.09 0.10 0.11

(c) 1.25 1.26 1.27 1.28 1.29 1.30 1.31

(d) 1.78 1.79 1.80 1.81 1.82 1.83 1.84

(e) 25.27 25.28 25.29 25.30 25.31 25.32 25.33

(f) 32.98 32.99 33.00 33.01 33.02 33.03 33.04

3 (a) 0.07   (c) 1.26   (e) 23.73

(b) 0.11   (d) 1.86   (f) 13.03

4 (a) 0.09 0.08 0.07 0.06 0.05 0.04 0.03

(b) 1.08 1.07 1.06 1.05 1.04 1.03 1.02

(c) 1.02 1.01 1.00 0.99 0.98 0.97 0.96

(d) 5.15 5.14 5.13 5.12 5.11 5.10 5.09

(e) 26.73 26.72 26.71 26.70 26.69 26.68 26.67

(f) 47.03 47.02 47.01 47.00 46.99 46.98 46.97

5 (a) 0.03   (c) 1.12   (e) 26.65

(b) 1.02   (d) 5.11   (f) 53.95

Exercise 17.4 Ordering decimals – tenths and hundredths

1 (a) 0.8   (c) 0.5   (e) 0.75

(b) 0.62   (d) 0.7

2 (a) 0.2   (c) 0.21   (e) 0.01

(b) 0.49   (d) 0.05

Exercise 17.5 Ordering decimals – thousandths

1 (a) 0.5   0.6   0.7

(b) 0.71   0.73   0.74

(c) 0.8	0.82	0.87		(g) 0.09	0.123	0.14	0.25
(d) 0.502	0.55	0.6		(h) 0.012	0.102	0.12	0.21
(e) 0.07	0.62	0.7		(i) 0.054	0.45	0.504	0.54
(f) 0.17	0.32	0.406	0.5	(j) 0.17	0.71	1.07	7.1
2 (a) 0.19	0.16	0.15		(f) 0.8	0.41	0.306	0.17
(b) 0.68	0.66	0.64		(g) 0.242	0.1	0.09	0.07
(c) 0.31	0.3	0.29		(h) 0.63	0.603	0.36	0.063
(d) 0.97	0.2	0.106		(i) 0.491	0.419	0.194	0.149
(e) 0.201	0.102	0.021		(j) 213	21.3	2.13	0.213

Exercise 17.6 Writing decimals as fractions

1 $\dfrac{3}{10}$

2 $\dfrac{61}{100}$

3 $\dfrac{127}{1000}$

4 $\dfrac{77}{100}$

5 $\dfrac{707}{1000}$

6 $\dfrac{7}{10}$

7 $4\dfrac{23}{100}$

8 $62\dfrac{83}{100}$

9 $1\dfrac{369}{1000}$

Exercise 17.7 Lowest terms

1 $\dfrac{3}{5}$

2 $\dfrac{4}{5}$

3 $\dfrac{1}{2}$

4 $\dfrac{7}{50}$

5 $\dfrac{3}{25}$

6 $\dfrac{3}{20}$

7 $\dfrac{1}{4}$

8 $\dfrac{9}{50}$

9 $\dfrac{23}{50}$

10 $\dfrac{4}{25}$

11 $\dfrac{7}{20}$

12 $\dfrac{31}{50}$

13 $\dfrac{11}{25}$

14 $\dfrac{9}{20}$

15 $\dfrac{8}{25}$

16 $\dfrac{37}{50}$

17 $\dfrac{6}{25}$

18 $\dfrac{19}{20}$

19 $\dfrac{3}{4}$

20 $\dfrac{1}{50}$

21 $\dfrac{1}{25}$

22 $\dfrac{1}{20}$

23 $3\dfrac{1}{5}$

24 $1\dfrac{13}{50}$

Exercise 17.8 Rounding to the nearest whole number

1 (a) 9   (b) 7   (c) 3   (d) 6   (e) 3

2 3 kg

3 7 °C

4 11 s

5 2 m

6 £27

7 49 cm

8 37 °C, 98 °F

9 8 litres

10 124 cm

Exercise 17.9 Summary

1. (a) $\frac{9}{100}$ (b) 20 (c) $\frac{7}{1000}$ (d) $\frac{3}{10}$ (e) 6

2. (a) (i) 0.4, 0.5, 0.6, 0.7, 0.8, 0.9, 1.0, 1.1, 1.2
   (ii) 2.4, 2.3, 2.2, 2.1, 2.0, 1.9, 1.8, 1.7, 1.6, 1.5
   (b) (i) 0.05, 0.06, 0.07, 0.08, 0.09, 0.10, 0.11, 0.12, 0.13
   (ii) 2.64, 2.63, 2.62, 2.61, 2.60, 2.59, 2.58, 2.57

3. (a) 0.9, 0.86, 0.75, 0.72
   (b) 0.33, 0.32, 0.313, 0.033
   (c) 1.7, 0.79, 0.759, 0.7

4. (a) 0.45, 0.53, 0.69, 0.96
   (b) 0.004, 0.4, 0.426, 0.46
   (c) 3.15, 3.51, 5.23, 5.32

5. (a) $\frac{3}{5}$ (c) $\frac{31}{50}$ (e) $\frac{1}{4}$ (g) $\frac{2}{25}$
   (b) $\frac{3}{20}$ (d) $\frac{1}{2}$ (f) $\frac{11}{25}$ (h) $\frac{7}{10}$

6. (a) 6 (b) 18 (c) 45 (d) 8

Activity – Dominoes

Practical

Pupils can cut out the dominoes from the worksheet or you can challenge them to make their own.

A good introduction to this activity would be to play traditional dominoes. Pupils can then play this equivalent fraction and decimal version.

18 Calculating with decimals

This chapter follows the following elements of the National Curriculum for Year 4:

Number - Fractions (including decimals)

Programme of study (statutory requirements)
Pupils should be taught to:
- find the effect of dividing a one- or two-digit number by 10 and 100, identifying the value of the digits in the answer as units, tenths and hundredths
- count up and down in hundredths; recognise that hundredths arise when dividing an object by a hundred and dividing tenths by ten.
- compare numbers with the same number of decimal places up to two decimal places
- recognise and write decimal equivalents of any number of tenths or hundredths
- recognise and write decimal equivalents to $\frac{1}{4}$; $\frac{1}{2}$; $\frac{3}{4}$
- round decimals with one decimal place to the nearest whole number

Notes and guidance (non-statutory)
- Pupils' understanding of the number system and decimal place value is extended at this stage to tenths and then hundredths. This includes relating the decimal notation to division of whole numbers by 10 and later 100

This chapter also covers the following elements not listed in the National Curriculum programme of study KS2:

- Calculating with decimals
- Multiplying and dividing by 1000

Exercise 18.1 Adding decimals

1. 1.1
2. 3.6
3. 13.6
4. 2.7
5. 2.47
6. 3.93
7. 8.0
8. 14.2
9. 26.02
10. 34.3
11. 58.4
12. 88.5
13. 148.8
14. 48.3
15. 104.3
16. 11.7
17. 16.9
18. 13.5
19. 26.3
20. 2.2
21. 45.83
22. 44.75
23. 39.16
24. 19.314
25. 48.396
26. 65
27. 15.19
28. 15.8
29. 181.2
30. 558.33

Exercise 18.2 Subtracting decimals

1 3.4
2 4.4
3 0.6
4 1.18
5 4.85
6 6.67
7 31.7
8 25.2
9 16.7
10 9.2
11 6.65
12 28.2
13 4.13
14 12.7
15 2.73
16 1.96
17 24.9
18 3.32
19 1.07
20 4.146
21 21.18
22 91.63
23 1.842
24 66.6
25 32.178
26 17.63
27 5.53
28 0.364
29 232.2
30 1.629

Exercise 18.3 Multiplying decimals by 10, 100 and 1000

1 (a) 43
   (b) 286.4
   (c) 1.9
   (d) 8

2 (a) 463.2
   (b) 386
   (c) 87.2
   (d) 4.23
   (e) 0.16
   (f) 170

3 (a) 1295
   (b) 326.7
   (c) 12 329
   (d) 87
   (e) 400
   (f) 23 420
   (g) 240
   (h) 365

4 (a) 17.5
   (b) 338
   (c) 2550
   (d) 8
   (e) 0.7
   (f) 142.5
   (g) 345
   (h) 1.4
   (i) 10
   (j) 1
   (k) 2720
   (l) 0.6
   (m) 7050
   (n) 840
   (o) 387.5
   (p) 2600
   (q) 29.5
   (r) 4.05

Exercise 18.4 Dividing decimals by 10, 100 and 1000

1 (a) 1.86
   (b) 0.63
   (c) 1.9
   (d) 83.5
   (e) 230
   (f) 0.3

2 (a) 1.482
   (b) 0.387
   (c) 17
   (d) 3.65
   (e) 151.3
   (f) 0.62
   (g) 0.064
   (h) 0.09

3 (a) 4.865
   (b) 27.9
   (c) 0.7875
   (d) 2.5
   (e) 0.425
   (f) 0.005
   (g) 0.0184
   (h) 0.0072

4 (a) 3.24
   (b) 1.234
   (c) 3.2179
   (d) 29.8
   (e) 3.5
   (f) 2.756
   (g) 28.74
   (h) 0.78

(i) 0.83   (m) 0.284   (q) 0.0355   (u) 0.027
(j) 0.409   (n) 0.06   (r) 0.046   (v) 0.0004
(k) 0.6   (o) 0.0015   (s) 0.009   (w) 0.007
(l) 0.5   (p) 0.008   (t) 0.0002

Exercise 18.5 Summary

1 (a) 7.33   (c) 53.1   (e) 50.93
  (b) 27.27   (d) 26.5

2 (a) 16.7   (c) 33.8   (e) 76.5
  (b) 33.77   (d) 6.35

3 (a) 4.8   (c) 9.1   (e) 8.4
  (b) 5.4   (d) 2.8   (f) 74.6

4 (a) 650   (c) 286   (e) 875
  (b) 7   (d) 491.5   (f) 28 900

5 (a) 3.3   (c) 57.8   (e) 1.247
  (b) 0.006   (d) 0.27   (f) 0.009

Activity - Mrs Chick's puzzle

5 baskets and 36 eggs

If you put 7 eggs in each of 5 baskets, there is 1 egg left over.

If you put 9 eggs in a basket, you fill 4 baskets exactly.

19 Metric measurement

This chapter follows the following elements of the National Curriculum for Year 4:

Number - Fractions

Programme of study (statutory requirements)
Pupils should be taught to:
- solve problems involving increasingly harder fractions to calculate quantities, and fractions to divide quantities, including non-unit fractions where the answer is a whole number
- solve simple measure problems involving fractions and decimals to two decimal places

Notes and guidance (non-statutory)
- Pupils learn decimal notation and the language associated with it, including in the context of measurements. They build on their understanding of place value and decimal notation to record metric measures.
- Pupils understand the relation between non-unit fractions and multiplication and division of quantities, with particular emphasis on tenths and hundredths.
- They make comparisons and order decimal amounts and quantities that are expressed to the same number of decimal places.

Measurement

Programme of study (statutory requirements)
Pupils should be taught to:
- convert between different units of measure (e.g. kilometre to metre; hour to minute)
- solve problems involving increasingly harder fractions to calculate quantities, and fractions to divide quantities, including non-unit fractions where the answer is a whole number
- estimate, compare and calculate different measures

Notes and guidance (non-statutory)
- They use multiplication to convert from larger to smaller units.

■ Notes

- Start the chapter with some practical measuring.
- Pupils should know already what a centimetre looks like from their rulers, but they will gain a better idea of a metre from measuring their own heights.
- Mass can be a harder concept to visualise, but picking up masses of different sizes and weighing themselves will all help.
- Pupils will probably have some concept of what a litre looks like. Ask them to use this to estimate their own volume. Encourage discussion of how they could do this.

Exercise 19.1 Measuring lines

1. 9.5 cm
2. 5.3 cm
3. 8.7 cm
4. 4.8 cm
5. 7.4 cm
6. 11.9 cm
7. 10.0 cm
8. 6.1 cm
9. 9.2 cm
10. 3.6 cm

Exercise 19.2 Drawing lines
Check pupils' drawings

Exercise 19.3 Converting units of length 1

1. (a) 80 mm (b) 150 mm (c) 68 mm (d) 32.5 mm (e) 5 mm
2. (a) 200 cm (b) 1500 cm (c) 475 cm (d) 2700 cm (e) 500 cm
3. (a) 3000 mm (b) 2500 mm (c) 4750 mm (d) 7900 mm (e) 500 mm
4. (a) 8000 m (b) 25 000 m (c) 4750 m (d) 7900 m (e) 500 m
5. (a) 70 mm (b) 3000 mm (c) 600 m (d) 6000 mm (e) 88 cm (f) 430 cm (g) 85 cm (h) 11 600 m (i) 750 mm (j) 120 mm

Exercise 19.4 Converting units of length 2

1. (a) 6 cm (b) 3.8 cm (c) 30 cm (d) 0.8 cm
2. (a) 7 m (b) 12.5 m (c) 0.3 m (d) 0.07 m
3. (a) 9 m (b) 5.5 m (c) 0.75 m (d) 0.085 m
4. (a) 3 km (b) 25 km (c) 0.4 km (d) 0.11 km
5. (a) 0.25 m (b) 12 km (c) 0.745 m (d) 7.5 cm (e) 1.5 km (f) 1.27 m (g) 0.08 km (h) 2.8 m (i) 0.1 cm (j) 0.01 m

Exercise 19.5 Converting units of mass 1

1. (a) 2000 mg (b) 12 000 mg (c) 3500 mg (d) 600 mg
2. (a) 6000 g (b) 14 200 g (c) 800 g (d) 5350 g
3. (a) 3000 kg (b) 6700 kg (c) 250 kg (d) 12 000 kg
4. (a) 6000 mg (b) 8000 g (c) 15 000 kg (d) 2750 g (e) 7125 kg (f) 600 mg (g) 1700 kg (h) 10 500 mg (i) 385 g (j) 80 kg

Exercise 19.6 Converting units of mass 2

1. (a) 6 g (b) 3.7 g (c) 12 g (d) 0.95 g
2. (a) 2 kg (b) 1.4 kg (c) 0.575 kg (d) 0.05 kg
3. (a) 3 t (b) 1.02 t (c) 0.7 t (d) 120 t
4. (a) 9 t (c) 15 g (e) 0.454 kg (g) 0.4 t (i) 0.1 kg
   (b) 1.2 kg (d) 5.05 t (f) 1.85 g (h) 0.05 t (j) 0.01 g

Exercise 19.7 Converting units of capacity

1. (a) 5000 ml (b) 7500 ml (c) 330 ml (d) 12 000 ml
2. (a) 9 l (b) 1.3 l (c) 0.4 l (d) 50.5 l

Exercise 19.8 Fractions of metric quantities

1. (a) 500 ml (c) 750 g (e) 500 kg
   (b) 25 cm (d) 1 mm (f) 750 m
2. (a) 100 mg (c) 250 mg
   (b) 500 mg (d) 750 mg
3. (a) 300 ml (c) 900 g (e) 600 kg
   (b) 70 cm (d) 4 mm (f) 800 m
4. (a) 75 cm (c) 200 kg (e) 1500 m or 1.5 km
   (b) 3000 g or 3 kg (d) 600 ml (f) 15 mm or 1.5 cm

Exercise 19.9 Calculating a fraction of a metric quantity

1. (a) 3 l (c) 5 kg (e) 2 t
   (b) 5 m (d) 55 cm (f) 0.5 km
2. (a) 150 g (c) 45 l (e) 18 cm
   (b) 54 t (d) 140 m (f) 76 kg
3. (a) 0.2 t (c) 0.3 cm (e) 0.2 km
   (b) 0.05 l (d) 0.8 kg (f) 0.4 m
4. (a) 1500 ml (c) 150 g (e) 150 cm
   (b) 2100 m (e) 15 mm (f) 2750 ml

Exercise 19.10 Ordering decimal amounts

1. (a) 103 cm = 1.03 m (c) 750 ml > 0.7 l (e) 3300 kg = 3.3 t
   (b) 225 g < 0.3 kg (d) 45 mm < 5 cm (f) 8 km > 850 m
2. (a) 1.02 m   1.2 m   1.21 m   1.25 m
   (b) 0.033 kg   0.3 kg   0.303 kg   0.33 kg

(c) 0.066 l   0.6 l   0.606 l   0.66 l
(d) 3.03 cm   3.33 cm   3.5 cm   36 mm
(e) 10.05 g   10.5 g   10 550 mg   10.555 g
(f) 0.9 km   990 m   9 km   9100 m

3 My sister   4 The red apple   5 My brother's bottle

Exercise 19.11 Problem solving

1 (a) 1600 m
  (b) 1.6 km
2 20 m
3 15 staples
4 (a) 1575 g
  (b) 1.575 kg
5 840 g

6 125 g
7 (a) 3500 kg
  (b) 3.5 t
8 30 l
9 19 times
10 300 ml more

Exercise 19.12 Summary

1 (a) 48 mm   (k) 0.9 kg
  (b) 500 cm   (l) 13.5 g
  (c) 1500 mm   (m) 0.8 km
  (d) 10 800 m   (n) 1.2 m
  (e) 4000 mg   (o) 0.5 m
  (f) 3750 g   (p) 8.5 cm
  (g) 600 kg   (q) 1.3 m
  (h) 6875 ml   (r) 13 cm
  (i) 0.04 l   (s) 0.01 kg
  (j) 43 t   (t) 10 000 g

2 (a) 4 l   (b) 2 kg   (c) 35 km   (d) 375 g
3 (a) 0.4 cm   (b) 0.07 m   (c) 1.2 t   (d) 0.14 l
4 (a) 500 g   (b) 15 mm   (c) 60 m   (d) 3500 ml
5 (a) 1400 g   (b) 1.4 kg
6 28 cm
7 (a) 22.5 mm   (b) 2.25 cm
8 (a) 25 coins   (b) £12.50
9 (a) 6 l   (b) 24 glasses
10 Yes, with 5 mm spare

Activity – Traffic control

1. (a) 3   (b) 3

2.

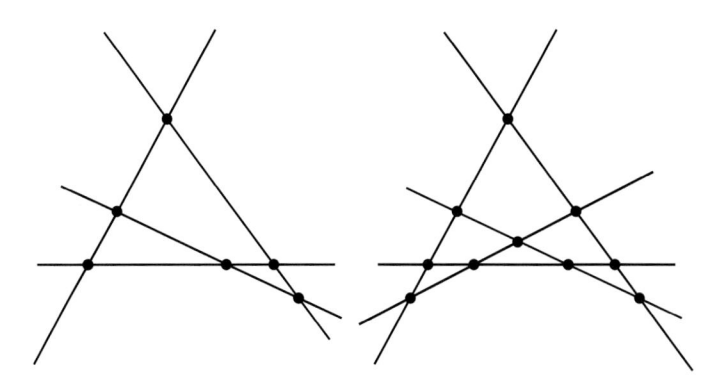

3.

Streets	Policemen
1	0
2	1
3	3
4	6
5	10

4. The numbers in the 'policemen' column are the triangular numbers. Add 1 to the first number (0), then add 2, then 3, then 4, and so on.

5. (a) 15   (b) 21

20 Angles and direction

This chapter follows the following elements of the National Curriculum for Year 4:

Geometry - Properties of shapes

Programme of study (statutory requirements)
Pupils should be taught to:
- identify acute and obtuse angles and compare and order angles up to two right angles by size

Notes and guidance (non-statutory)
- Pupils compare and order angles in preparation for using a protractor.

This chapter also covers the following elements not listed in the National Curriculum programme of study KS3:
- Measuring angles
- Drawing angles

■ Notes

■ Measuring angles is not on the National Curriculum until Year 5, when pupils are required to measure all angles, including reflex angles. You may wish to introduce measuring angles that are a multiple of 10° in Year 4 to introduce this skill more gradually.

Exercise 20.1 Types of angle

1. acute
2. acute
3. right
4. obtuse
5. obtuse
6. acute
7. right
8. acute
9. obtuse
10. acute
11. obtuse
12. acute
13. 1 is the smallest
14. 9 is the largest
15. 1 2 6 3 4 5
16. 9 11 7 12 8 10

Exercise 20.2 Measuring angles

1. 40°
2. 60°
3. 30°
4. 70°
5. 110°
6. 140°
7. 130°
8. 120°
9. 50°
10. 100°
11. 100°
12. 80°

Exercise 20.3 Drawing angles

Measure pupils' angles

Exercise 20.4 Angles and the hands of a clock
1 (a) 60°　　(b) 90°　　(c) 210°　　(d) 300°　　(e) 15°
2 (a) 30°　　(b) 90°　　(c) 150°　　(d) 180°　　(e) 45°

Exercise 20.5 Angles and the compass
1 (a) 45°　　(e) 135°　　(i) 90°　　(m) 180°
　(b) 135°　 (f) 225°　　(j) 90°　　(n) 180°
　(c) 225°　 (g) 45°　　 (k) 90°　　(o) 270°
　(d) 315°　 (h) 135°　　(l) 90°

Exercise 20.6 Directions on a grid

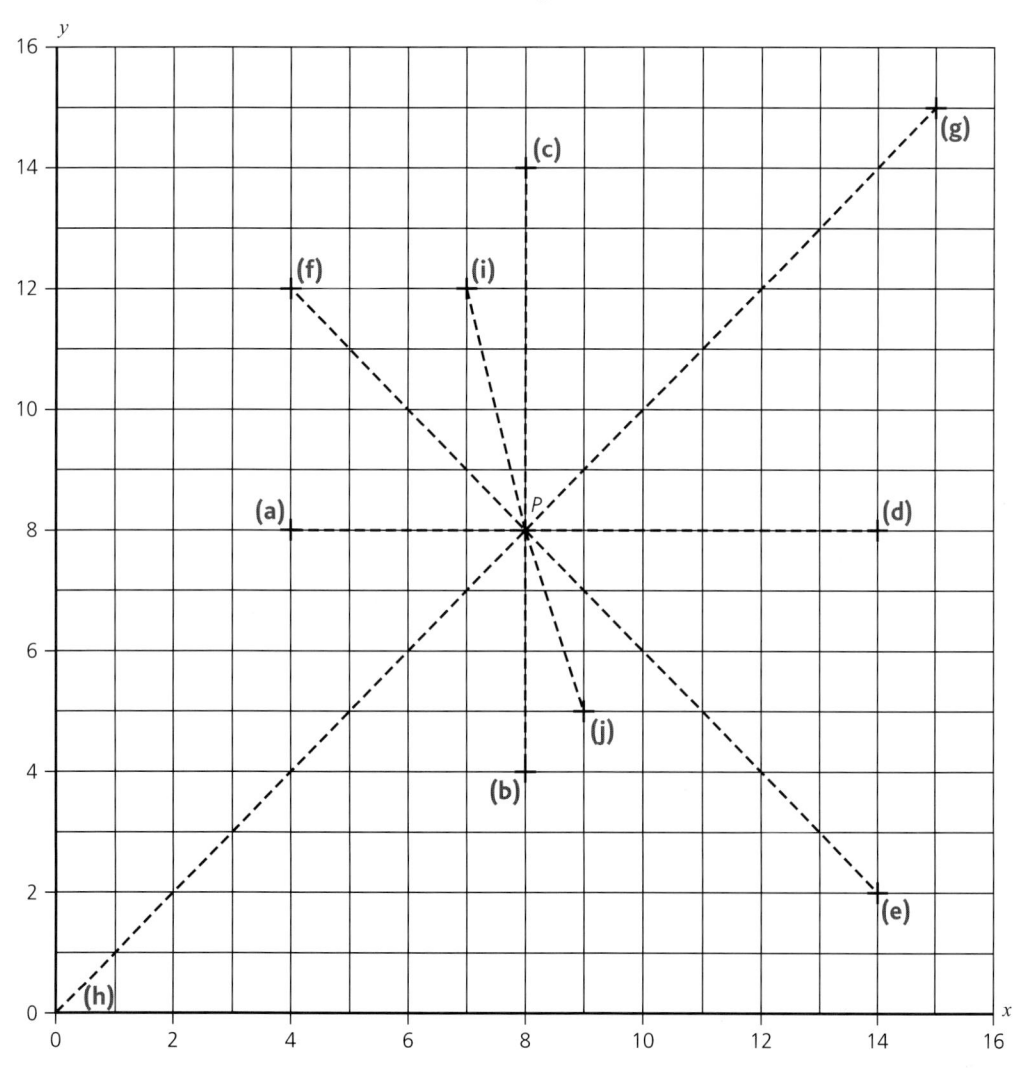

1 (a) 4 squares west
  (b) 4 squares south
  (c) 6 squares north
  (d) 6 squares east
  (e) 6 squares south-east
  (f) 4 squares north-west
  (g) 7 squares north-east
  (h) 8 squares south-west
  (i) 4 squares north, 1 square west or vice versa
  (j) 3 squares south, 1 square east or vice versa

Exercise 20.7 Summary

1 (a) 80°   (b) 100°   (c) 40°   (d) 130°

2 Check pupils' answers

3 (a) 45°   (b) 135°

4 (a) (3, 6)   (c) (7, 2)   (e) 6 squares north-east
  (b) (0, 6)   (d) 5 squares south

Activity – Clock shapes

Shape 1

Shape 2

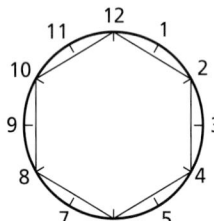

Shape 3

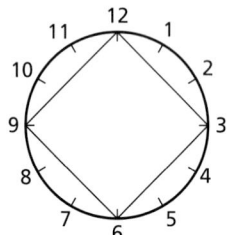

Shape 4

Shape 5

Shape 6

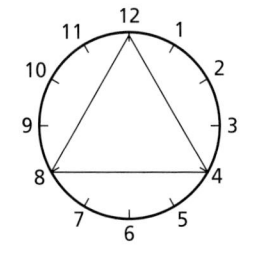

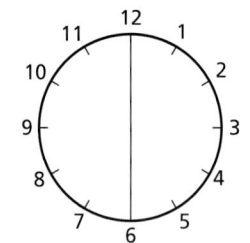

Shape 7

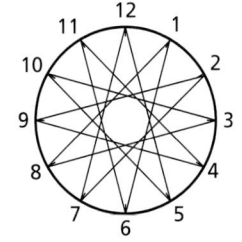

Shapes 5 and 7 are the same.

Shape 8 will be the same as shape 4, shape 9 will be the same as shape 3…

Money 21

This chapter follows the following elements of the National Curriculum for Year 4:

Number - Fractions

Programme of study (statutory requirements)
Pupils should be taught to:
- solve simple measure and money problems involving fractions and decimals to two decimal places.
- estimate, compare and calculate different measures, including money in pounds and pence
- solve simple measure and money problems involving decimals to two decimal places

Measurement

Programme of study (statutory requirements)
Pupils should be taught to:
- estimate, compare and calculate different measures

Notes and guidance (non-statutory)
- Pupils build on their understanding of place value and decimal notation to record metric measures, including money.
- They use multiplication to convert from larger to smaller units.

■ Notes

■ You may wish to do this chapter before Chapter 17 Decimals as many pupils instinctively grasp the concept of money. This helps them to understand decimals.

Exercise 21.1 Conversion of money

1. (a) 400p   (d) 135p   (g) 40p   (j) 10 000c
   (b) 700c   (e) 625c   (h) 95c   (k) 5000c
   (c) 1200c (f) 2415c (i) 8c   (l) 200 000p

2. (a) £9   (d) £6.65 (g) £0.95 (j) £1.04
   (b) €8   (e) €1.48 (h) €0.05 (k) €1.40
   (c) $17   (f) $9.50 (i) $0.10 (l) $4.10

Exercise 21.2 Addition of money

1. 79p
2. £1.33
3. £1.16
4. 67p
5. £1.27
6. 93p
7. £1.90
8. £2.23
9. £2.42
10. £3.50
11. £4.69
12. £8.25
13. £9.85
14. $8.50
15. $15.15
16. £31.18

17	€6.75	21	£33.51	25	$22.30	29	€35.26
18	€36.24	22	€23.26	26	£5.11	30	$4.02
19	£6.75	23	£3.25	27	€2		
20	£9.93	24	£4.23	28	£7.48		

Exercise 21.3 Subtraction of money

1	£1.61	6	€2.84	11	£2.57	16	£8.73
2	£5.23	7	£1.61	12	£6.55	17	$22.70
3	£1.58	8	$1.84	13	£4.63	18	£21.60
4	£4.48	9	£2.63	14	€5.72	19	£45.64
5	£6.48	10	£3.58	15	£22.75	20	€62.71

Exercise 21.4 Multiplication of money

1	51p	9	£5.81	17	£53.92	25	£156.90
2	£1.52	10	£3.92	18	€76.68	26	$190.40
3	£3.65	11	£6.94	19	£92.50	27	£534.20
4	£2.52	12	£4.02	20	$10.92	28	€430.90
5	£6.72	13	$16.76	21	£57	29	£205.96
6	£5.12	14	£38.15	22	$52.20	30	$311.90
7	£2.52	15	€33.42	23	€82.50		
8	£5.70	16	£21.56	24	£43.50		

Exercise 21.5 Division of money

1	29p	9	12p	17	85p	25	£3.39
2	19p	10	47c	18	45p	26	£5.45
3	28c	11	89p	19	57c	27	€4.68
4	13p	12	57p	20	86p	28	£2.18
5	10c	13	66p	21	£1.88	29	£3.50
6	12p	14	87c	22	£1.29	30	$2.12
7	25c	15	59p	23	£2.63		
8	18p	16	75c	24	$2.47		

Exercise 21.6 Estimation

Pupils' answers could differ depending on their initial estimates.

1	£80	4	£80 000	7	10 tins
2	£3.20	5	£770 000	8	£25
3	£37	6	4 planes	9	£1880–£2050

Exercise 21.7 One-step problems

1. 62p
2. £3.55
3. £10.29
4. 41p
5. €11.75
6. 85p
7. £67.20
8. €349.80
9. $1.25
10. £9.40

Exercise 21.8 Two-step problems

1. 6 for 84p, save 24p
2. £405
3. £27.25
4. £3.75
5. £6.25
6. £2.40
7. €2.68
8. No, she is 30c short.
9. (a) £8.20
   (b) £11.80
10. £6.30

> **Activity – Money round the world**
>
> *Check pupils' answers.*
>
> This is a good opportunity for some cross-curricular work with Geography.
>
> In addition to researching different currencies, pupils could investigate how much things cost in other countries, for example a loaf of bread or a bottle of water. From this pupils will discover that other countries speak different languages. You could allocate a country to pupils and ask them to find out a number of facts. It would be a useful way of gathering information that could be used as data for techniques covered in the last chapter of this book.

22 Measurement and scales

This chapter follows the following elements of the National Curriculum for Year 4:

Number - Number and place value

Notes and guidance (non-statutory)
- They connect estimation and rounding numbers to the use of measuring instruments.

Measurement

Notes and guidance (non-statutory)
- They use multiplication to convert from larger to smaller units.

Exercise 22.1 Reading scales

1. A = 200   B = 500   C = 650
2. A = 400   B = 700   C = 850
3. A = 0.1   B = 0.6   C = 0.95
4. A = 0.8   B = 0.3   C = 0.15
5. A = 1200   B = 1450   C = 1725
6. A = 4200   B = 4500   C = 4850
7. A = 1.4   B = 1.7   C = 1.55
8. A = 4.4   B = 4.1   C = 4.75

Exercise 22.2 Reading scales on measuring instruments

1. (a) 1.5 kg   (b) 4.7 kg   (c) 0.6 kg
2. (a) 30 mph   (b) 74 mph   (c) 18 mph
3. (a) 15 °C   (b) 26 °C   (c) −6 °C   (d) 11 °C
4. (a) 300 g   (b) 1150 g   (c) 770 g
5. (a) 300 ml   (b) 450 ml   (c) 175 ml

Exercise 22.3 Marking numbers on a scale

1.

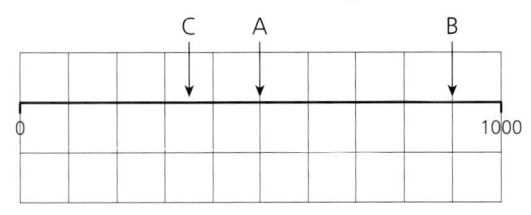

2.

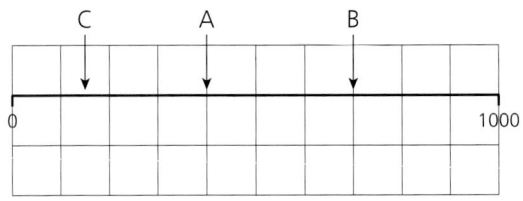

3 (scale 0 to 1000) B, A, C

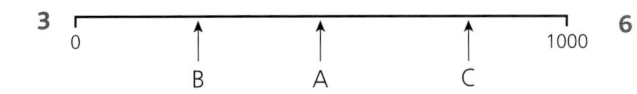

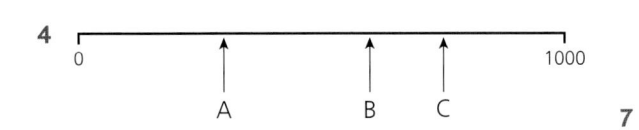

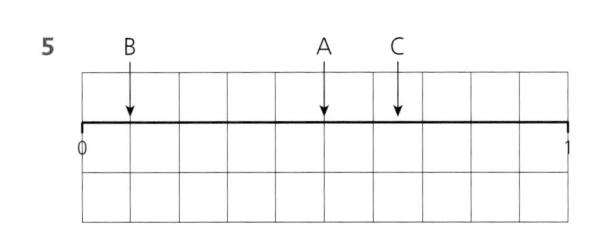

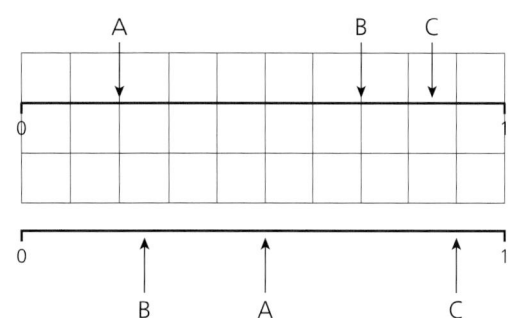

4 (scale 0 to 1000) A, B, C

5 (scale 0 to 1) B, A, C

6 (scale 0 to 1) A, B, C

7 (scale 0 to 1) B, A, C

8 (scale 0 to 1) A, B, C

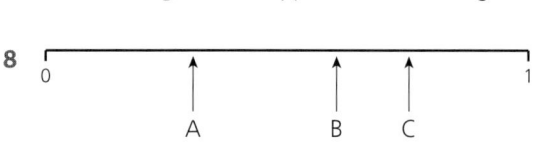

Exercise 22.4 Summary

1 (a) A = 0.5   B = 0.2   C = 0.85
   (b) A = 6   B = 1   C = 7.5
   (c) A = 40   B = 70   C = 15
   (d) A = 300   B = 450   C = 625
   (e) A = 3800   B = 3300   C = 3550
   (f) A = 6.4   B = 6.7   C = 6.25

2 (a) 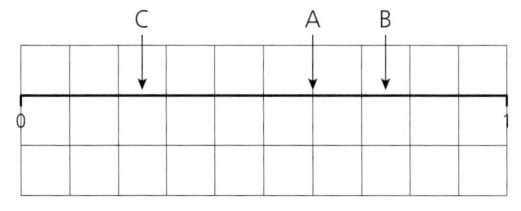 (scale 0 to 1) C, A, B
   (b) (scale 0 to 1) C, B, A
   (c) (scale 0 to 10) A, B, 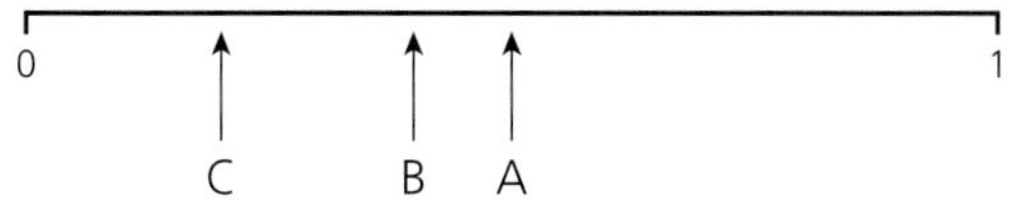 C 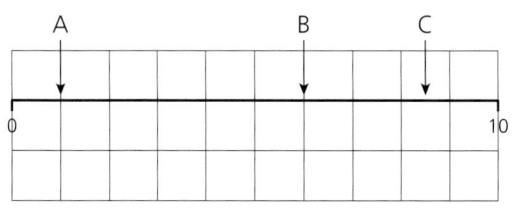
   (d) 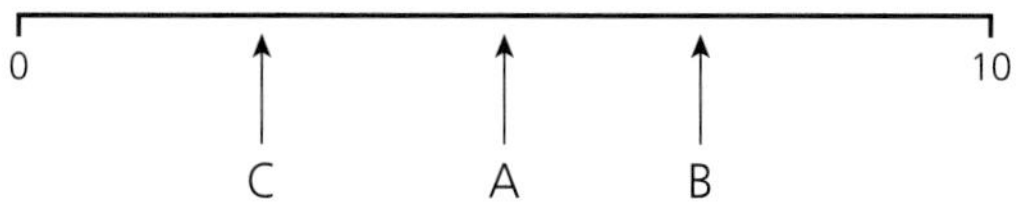 (scale 0 to 10) C, A, B
   (e) 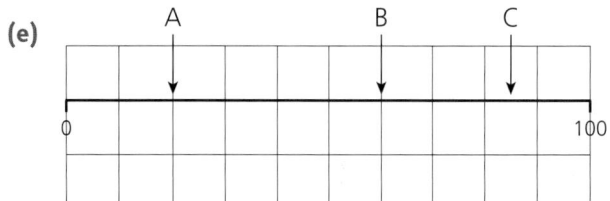 (scale 0 to 100) A, B, C
   (f) 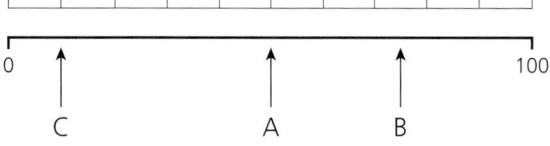 (scale 0 to 100) C, A, B
   (g) 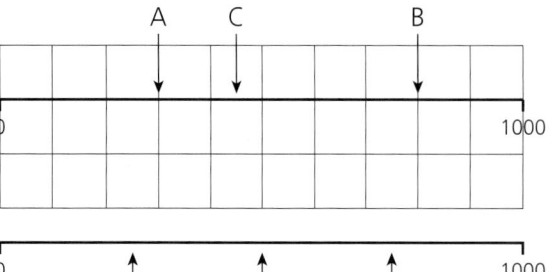 (scale 0 to 1000) A, C, B
   (h) 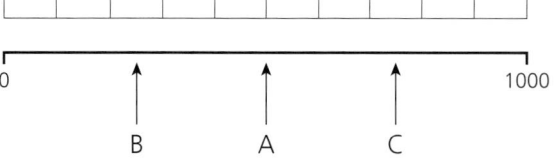 (scale 0 to 1000) B, A, C

3 (a) 53 kg   (b) 1.5 kg

Activity – Palindromes

For example:

1 stage:	18	24	35	42	53	63	72	81	90
2 stage:	19	37	49	57	64	75	82	93	
3 stage:	59	68	86	95					
4 stage:	69	78	87	96					

79 and 97 need 6 stages

89 and 98 need 24 stages

Don't forget single digits and numbers that repeat a digit (11, 22...) need 0 stages since they are palindromes to start with.

23 Perimeter and area

This chapter follows the following elements of the National Curriculum for Year 4:

Measurement

Programme of study (statutory requirements)
Pupils should be taught to:
- measure and calculate the perimeter of a rectilinear figure (including squares) in centimetres and metres
- find the area of rectilinear shapes by counting squares

Notes and guidance (non-statutory)
- Perimeter can be expressed algebraically as $2(a + b)$ where a and b are the dimensions in the same unit.
- They relate area to arrays and multiplication.

■ Notes

■ Although the National Curriculum expects pupils to find area by counting squares, the work in this chapter encourages them to think of the area of rectangular shapes in terms of arrays and multiplication.

Exercise 23.1 Perimeter

1 (a) 16 cm   (b) 20 cm   (c) 20 cm   (d) 28 cm
2 (a) 26 cm   (c) 80 cm   (e) 40 cm
   (b) 50 cm   (d) 20.8 cm
3 (a) 36 cm   (c) 80 cm   (e) 28.8 cm
   (b) 64 cm   (d) 18 cm   (f) 26.4 cm

Exercise 23.2 Calculating length and width

1

Perimeter	Length	Width
20 cm	6 cm	4 cm
36 cm	15 cm	3 cm
60 cm	20 cm	10 cm
48 cm	16 cm	8 cm
9 cm	3 cm	1.5 cm

2 (a) 4 cm   (b) 16 cm   (c) 25 cm   (d) 5.5 cm

Exercise 23.3 Area

1 15 cm²   5 16 cm²   9 13.5 cm²   13 8 cm²
2 24 cm²   6 26 cm²   10 20 cm²   14 18 cm²
3 9 cm²   7 24 cm²   11 15 cm²   15 63 cm²
4 25 cm²   8 18 cm²   12 10 cm²

Exercise 23.4 Area of a rectangle

1 15 m²   3 40 m²   5 24 m²   7 144 cm²
2 150 cm²   4 240 cm²   6 15 000 m²   8 64 m²

Summary exercise 23.5

1 (a) 24 cm²   (b) 16 cm²   (c) 18 cm²   (d) 22.5 cm²
2 28 cm   4 15 cm   6 8 cm
3 28 cm   5 15 cm   7 6 cm
8 (a) 56 m   (b) 180 m²

Activity – Same perimeter, different area

1 and 2 Shapes drawn with these dimensions, areas written inside the shapes.

11 cm × 1 cm	11 cm²	8 cm × 4 cm	32 cm²
10 cm × 2 cm	20 cm²	7 cm × 5 cm	35 cm²
9 cm × 3 cm	27 cm²	6 cm × 6 cm	36 cm²

3 36 cm²

4 a square

5 The largest area that can be enclosed by a rectangle with perimeter 40 cm is 100 cm² (a square of side 10 cm).

24 Tables, charts and graphs

This chapter follows the following elements of the National Curriculum for Year 4:
Statistics
Programme of study (statutory requirements)
Pupils should be taught to:
- interpret and present discrete and continuous data using appropriate graphical methods, including bar charts and time graphs
- solve comparison, sum and difference problems using information presented in bar charts, pictograms, tables and other graphs

Notes and guidance (non-statutory)
- Pupils understand and use a greater range of scales in their representations.
- Pupils begin to relate the graphical representation of data to recording change over time.

This chapter also covers the following elements not listed in the National Curriculum programme of study KS2:
- Frequency

■ Notes

■ Pupils are likely to engage more with this work if they use data collected from their own studies in science and geography.

Exercise 24.1 Reading from charts and tables

1 (a)

Number	Tally	Frequency
1	ⅢⅠ ⅢⅠ ⅠⅠ	12
2	ⅢⅠ ⅢⅠ	10
3	ⅢⅠ ⅠⅠ	7
4	ⅢⅠ ⅠⅠⅠⅠ	9
5	ⅢⅠ ⅢⅠ ⅠⅠⅠ	13
6	ⅢⅠ ⅢⅠ ⅠⅠⅠⅠ	14
	Total	65

   (b) 6   (c) 5 more   (d) 65

2 (a) Friday   (b) 25 people   (c) 15 more people

   (d) *For example*: They have just have been paid; they are in a good mood at end of the week.

3 (a) Blue House   (b) Green House   (c) 4 more   (d) 36 house points

4 (a)

Colour	Tally	Frequency
Blue	|||| ||	7
Green	||||	5
Orange	||	2
Pink	||||	4
Red	|||| |||	8
Yellow	|||	3
	Total	29

Year 4's favourite colours

Blue	☺ ☺ ☺ ⌣
Green	☺ ☺ ⌣
Orange	☺
Pink	☺ ☺
Red	☺ ☺ ☺ ☺
Yellow	☺ ⌣

☺ = 2 people   ⌣ = 1 person

(b) Yellow (c) Red (d) 1 child (e) 29 children

5 (a) Car (b) 10 children (c) 1 more child (d) 34 children

(e) *For example*: I think it is in the country as most children come by car which could be because they travel quite a long way to school.

6 (a) 2 flowers (b) Orange (c) 34 flowers

(d) *For example*: They are attractive to bees.

7 (a) April

(b) 10 more bicycles

(c) 52 bicycles

(d) *For example*: The weather may have been very wet.

8 (a)

Month	Tally	Frequency
January	IIII	4
February	III	3
March	IIII I	6
April	IIII IIII	10
May	IIII IIII IIII I	16
June	IIII IIII III	13
July	IIII IIII IIII IIII	19
August	IIII IIII I	11
September	IIII IIII IIII	14
October	IIII III	8
November	III	3
December	IIII IIII IIII	14
	Total	121

(b) (i) May, June and July

(ii) *For example*: Because the weather was warm and dry.

(c) (i) January, February and March

(ii) *For example*: Because the weather was cold and wet.

(d) People bought bicycles for Christmas presents.

Exercise 24.2 Drawing bar charts

1 (a)

Number of goals	Tally	Frequency
0	III	3
1	II	2
2	III	3
3	I	1
4	IIII	4
5	II	2
6	I	1
	Total	16

(b) **Number of goals scored by the netball team**

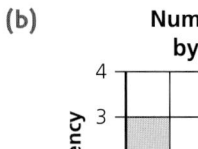

(c) 16

(d) 43

2 (a)

Type of fruit	Tally	Frequency
Apple	卌 I	6
Banana	卌 卌 I	11
Melon	卌 IIII	9
Orange	卌 卌	10
Strawberry	卌 卌 IIII	14
	Total	50

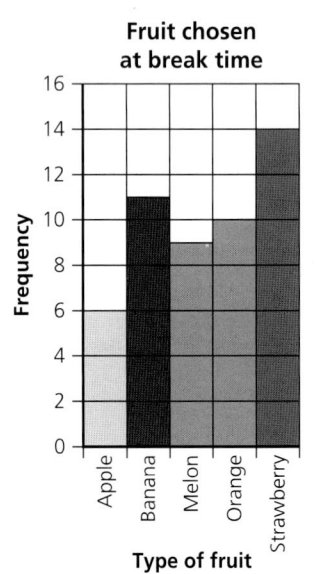

(b) **Fruit chosen at break time**

(c) Apple

(d) *For example*: The cook should buy fewer apples.

3 (a)

Amount of money (£)	Tally	Frequency
0	I	1
1	II	2
2	卌	5
3	卌	5
4	III	3
5	卌 IIII	9
6	III	3
	Total	28

(b) **Amount of money spent in shop**

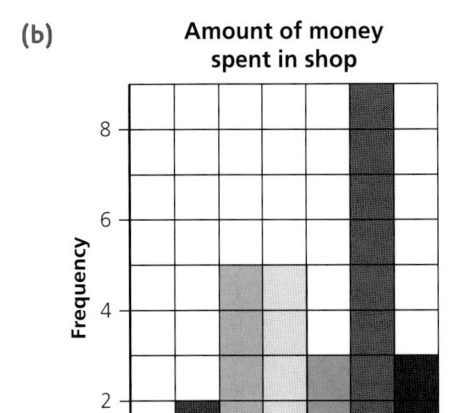

(c) *For example*: £5

(d) *For example*: He forgot to bring any money.

4 (a)

Country	Tally	Frequency
France	|||| |||| ||||	15
Italy	||||		6
Greece	|||| ||||	9
USA	|||| ||	7
Scotland	|||| ||||	10
Wales	||||	4
England	|||| ||||	9
	Total	60

(b) **Countries visited by Year 4**

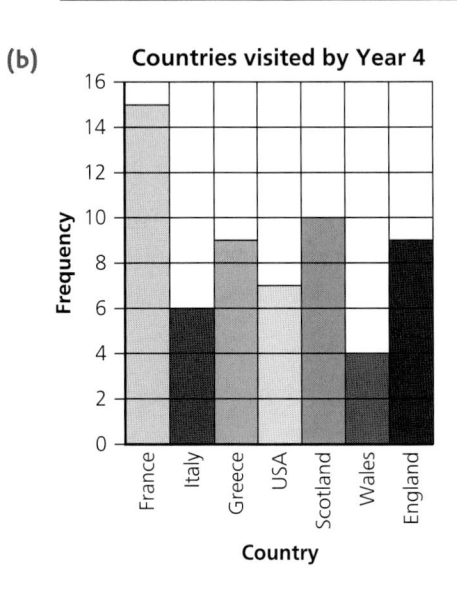

(c) *For example*: There was a school trip to France; it is easy to get there by ferry.

5 (a)

Pulse rate	Tally	Frequency
60–69	III	3
70–79	IIII I	6
80–89	IIII IIII I	11
90–99	IIII II	7
100–109	IIII	5
	Total	32

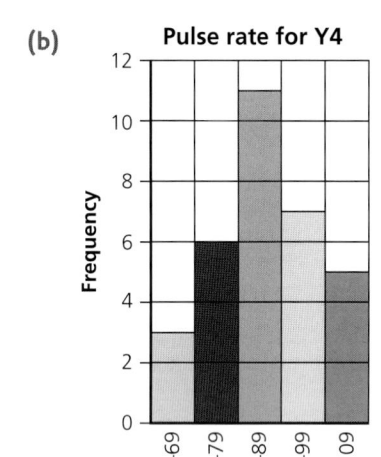

(b) Pulse rate for Y4 (bar chart with frequencies 3, 6, 11, 7, 5 for pulse rate ranges 60–69, 70–79, 80–89, 90–99, 100–109)

(c) *For example:* They had been running around.

Exercise 24.3 Reading line graphs

1 (a) 19.6 °C (d) 11 a.m. to 1 p.m.
 (b) 25 °C (e) 2 p.m.
 (c) 1 p.m.
 (f) *For example*: The outside temperature dropped; A window was opened.

2 (a) Day 14 (c) 4 cm (e) Day 18 and day 20
 (b) 7 cm (d) Day 8 and day 12

3 (a) Noon (b) 3 km (c) 2 hours (d) 1 hour
 (e) *For example*: They walked slower because they were looking at things on the way; They left the museum late so were made to walk faster.

4 (a) 5 hours (c) 10 km (e) Between 12.30 and 1 p.m. (g) 16 km
 (b) 1 hour (d) 30 minutes (f) (i) 5 km (h) 11.24 a.m. and 12.39 p.m.
   (ii) 12.5 km (*Accept close answers.*)

5 (a) 20 kg (c) June (e) *For example*: Sam was still not well.
 (b) August (d) 3.5 kg

Exercise 24.4 Drawing line graphs

1 (a) and (b)

(c) Day 2 and day 4

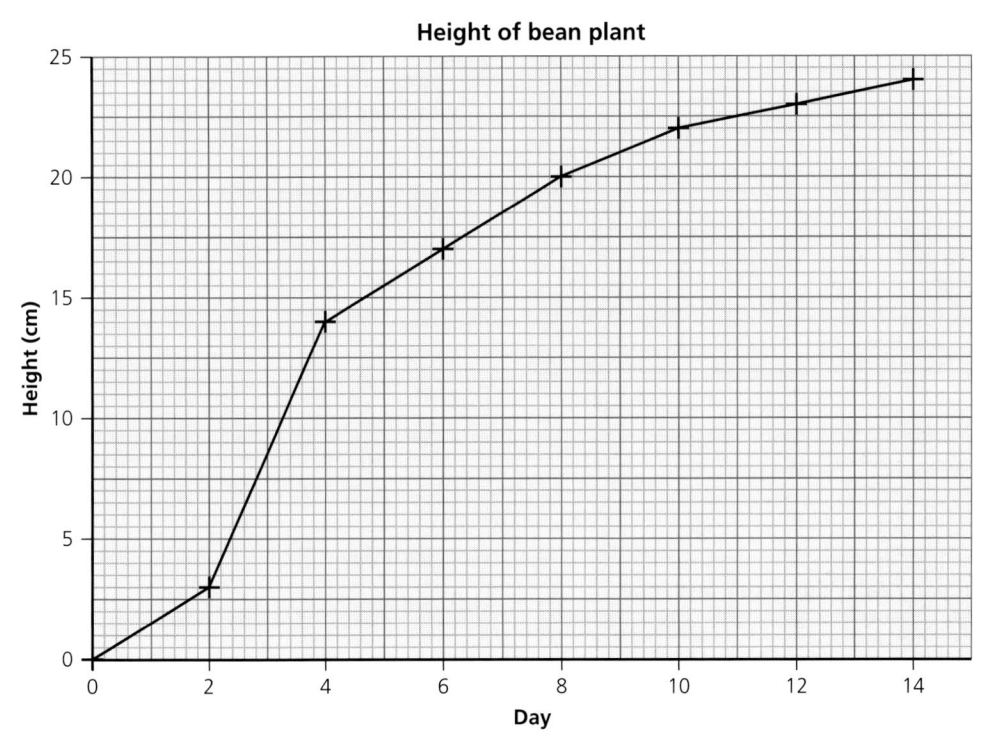

Height of bean plant

2 (a) and (b)

(c) Between 2 p.m. and 3 p.m.

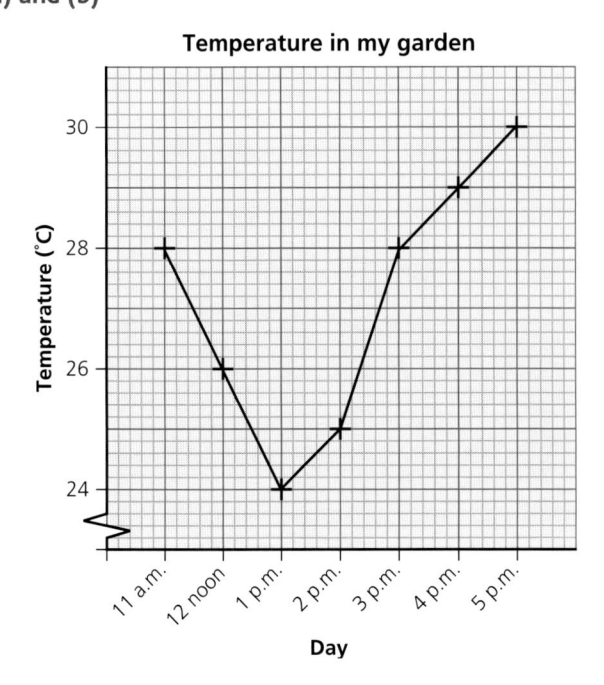

Temperature in my garden

3 (a) and (b)

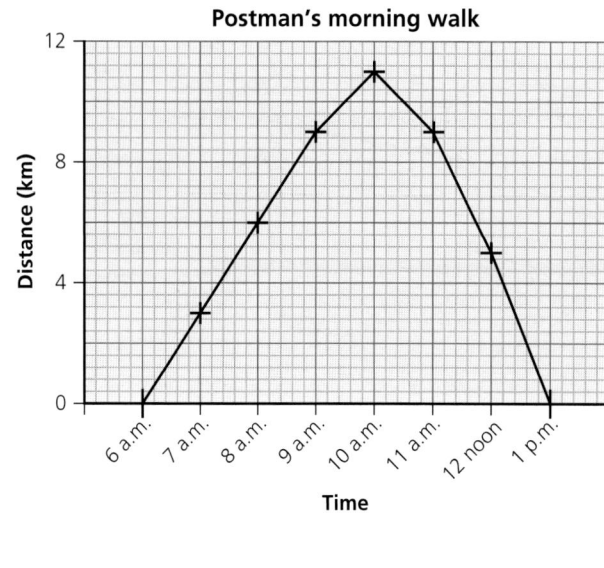

Postman's morning walk

(c) 10 a.m.

(d) 12 and 1 p.m.

(e) *For example*: He had no more letters to deliver; he hurried back to finish work.

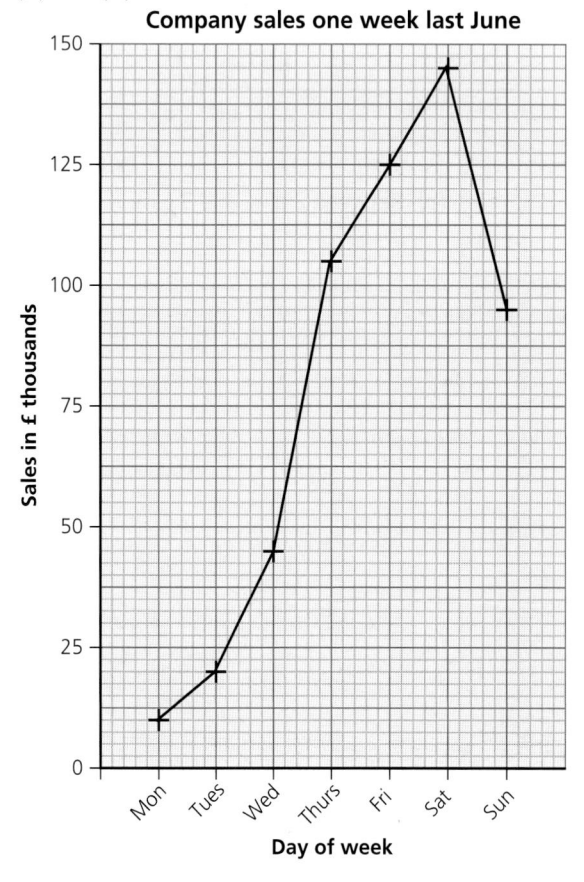

4 (a) and (b)

Company sales one week last June

(c) Saturday

(d) 3 days

Activity – A summer project

Practical work.

This activity provides another opportunity for some cross-curricular work with Science or Geography. If your pupils are going on an end of term trip you could ask them to devise some surveys or investigations. Many trips lend themselves to data collection, whether it is the choice of packed lunch sandwich fillings or the length of queues for attractions. With a bit of imagination there will plenty for them to research and data can be used in the classroom to draw charts and graphs.

Worksheet for Exercise 7.3

Name: _____ Class: _____ Date: _____

1 Plot and label these points on the grid.

A (5, 2)
B (8, 6)
C (4, 7)
D (1, 4)
E (3, 1)
F (7, 8)
G (0, 2)
H (2, 3)
I (6, 5)
J (7, 0)

2 Plot and label these points on the grid.

A (2, 4)
B (4, 7)
C (7, 2)
D (5, 1)
E (1, 5)
F (2, 0)
G (7, 8)
H (0, 6)
I (8, 3)
J (6, 5)

Worksheet for Exercise 7.4

Name: _____ Class: _____ Date: _____

Use one copy of this grid for questions 1 to 4 and another copy for questions 5 to 6

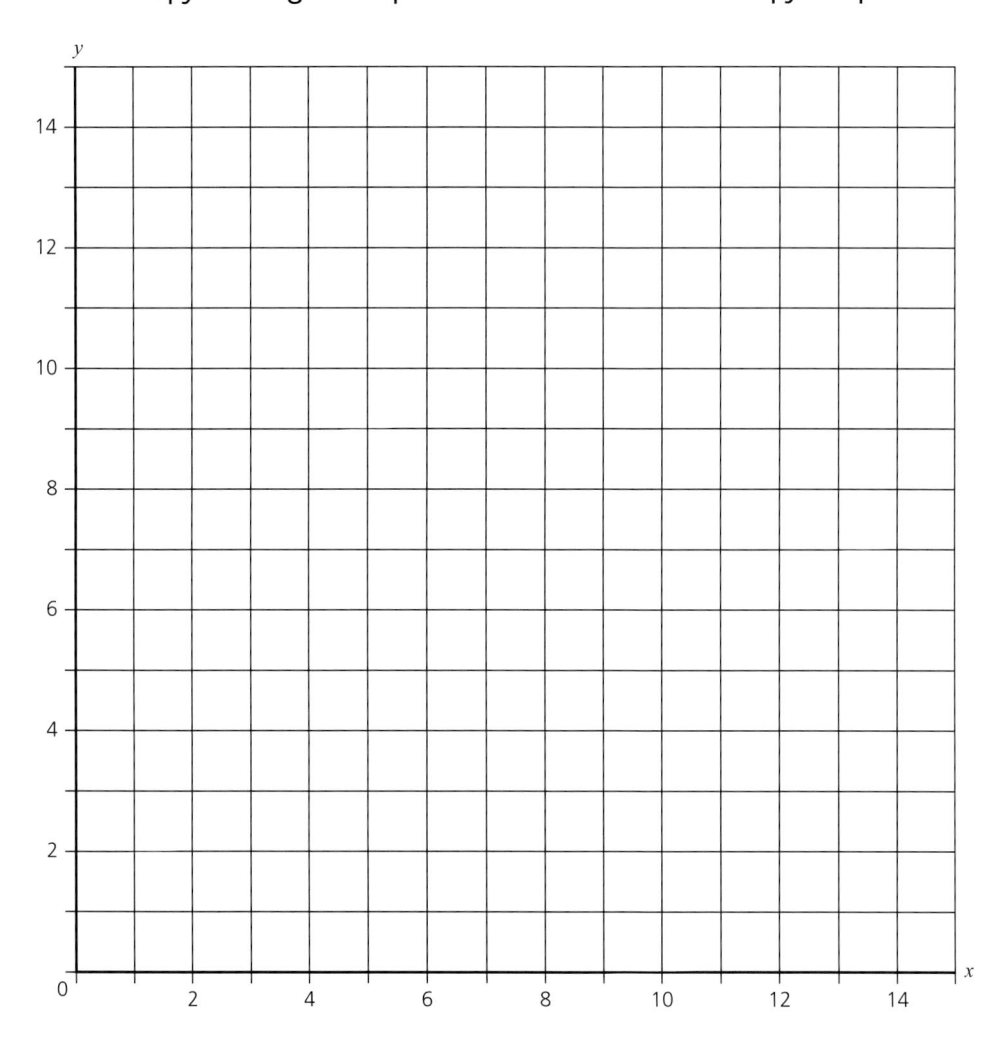

Worksheet for Exercise 7.5

Name: _____ Class: _____ Date: _____

Use one copy of this grid for questions 1 to 3, another copy for questions 5 to 8 and a copy for questions 9 to 10

Questions: _____

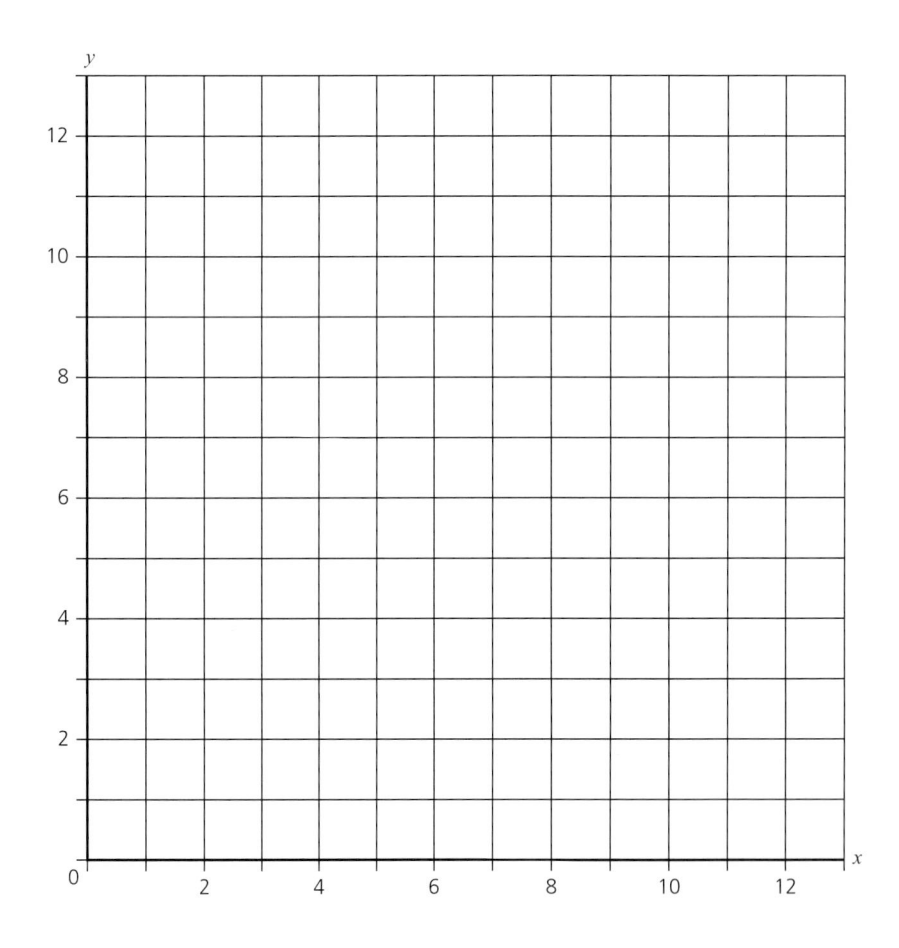

Worksheet for Exercise 7.7

Name: _____ Class: _____ Date: _____

For each question, draw the translation on the grid below and write down the co-ordinates of the image.

1 B _____   3 F _____   5 K _____   7 Q _____
2 D _____   4 H _____   6 M _____   8 S _____

Answer the rest of the questions in your exercise book.

Worksheet for Exercise 7.8

Name: _____ Class: _____ Date: _____

Answer question 1, question 6 and question 8 in your exercise book.

2   Plot and label these points on the grid below.

   A (4, 4)
   B (5, 8)
   C (2, 9)
   D (6, 3)
   E (3, 0)
   F (0, 8)

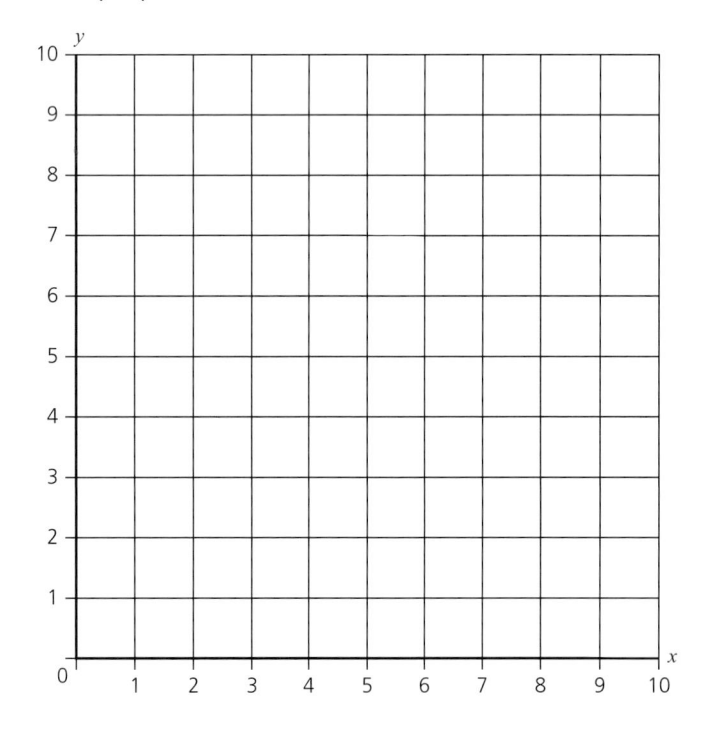

Name: _____ Class: _____ Date: _____

3 (a) Plot the points A (1, 5), B (6, 5) and C (1, 10)

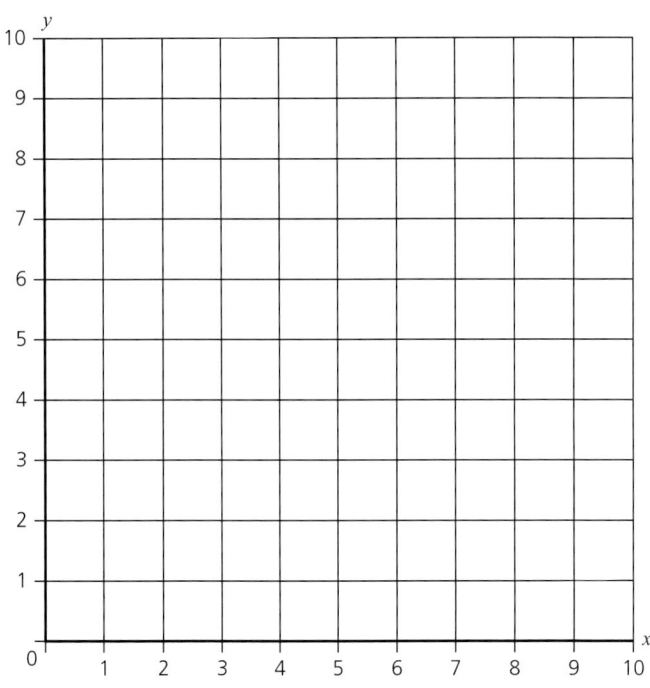

(b) Join the points, in order, to make triangle ABC

(c) Name the type of triangle you have drawn _____

4 (a) Plot the points P(4, 2), Q(7, 0), R(10, 2) and S(7, 4)

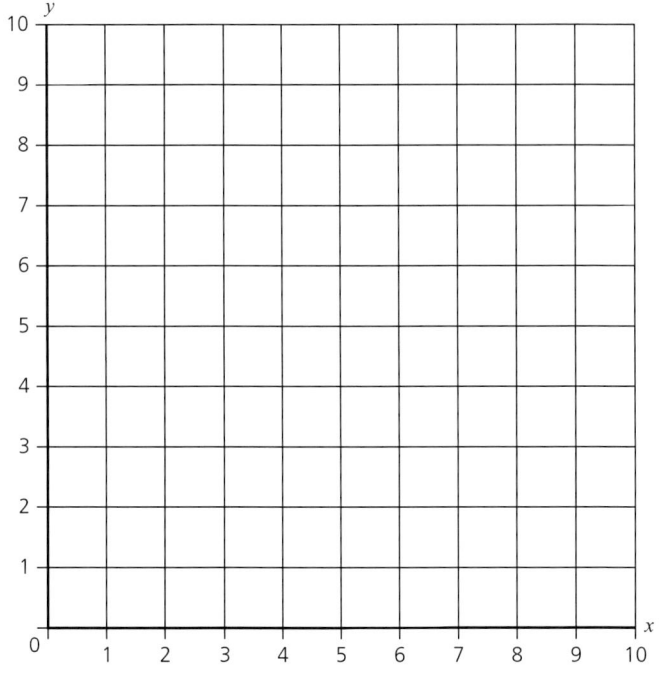

(b) Join the points, in order, to make quadrilateral PQRS.

(c) Name the type of quadrilateral you have drawn. _____

(d) Write down the co-ordinates of the point where its diagonals cross.

_____

Name: _____ Class: _____ Date: _____

5 (a) Plot the points W(6, 7), X(10, 7) and Y(10, 9)

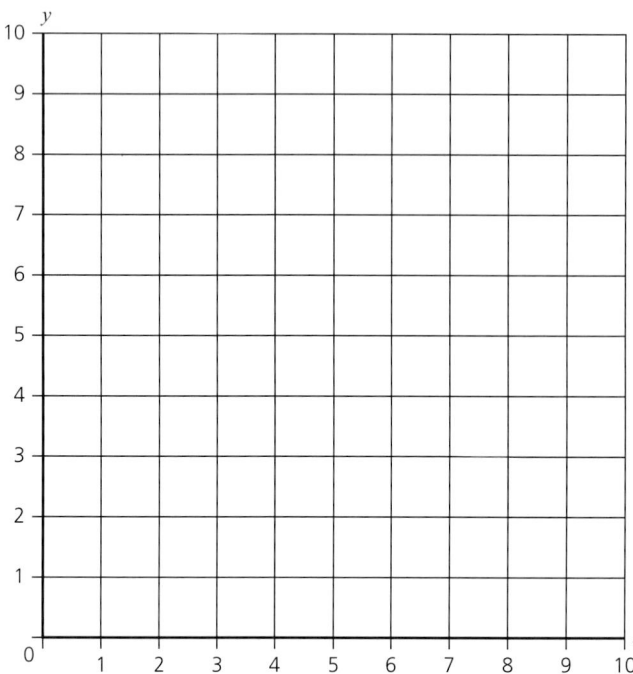

(b) Join W to X and X to Y

(c) Plot the point Z to make WXYZ a rectangle.

(d) Write down the co-ordinates of Z.
    _____

7 Draw each translation on the grid below and write down the co-ordinates of the image.

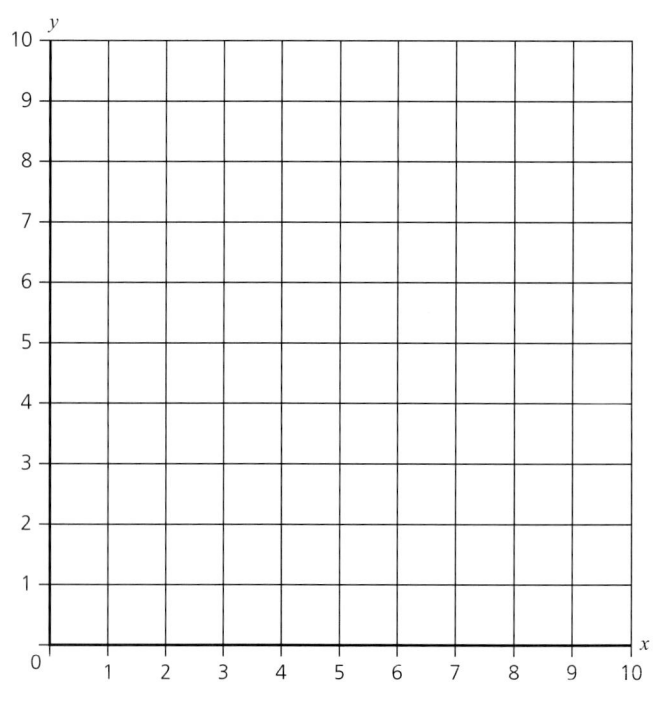

(a) B _____
(b) D _____
(c) F _____
(d) H _____

Worksheet for Activity 7

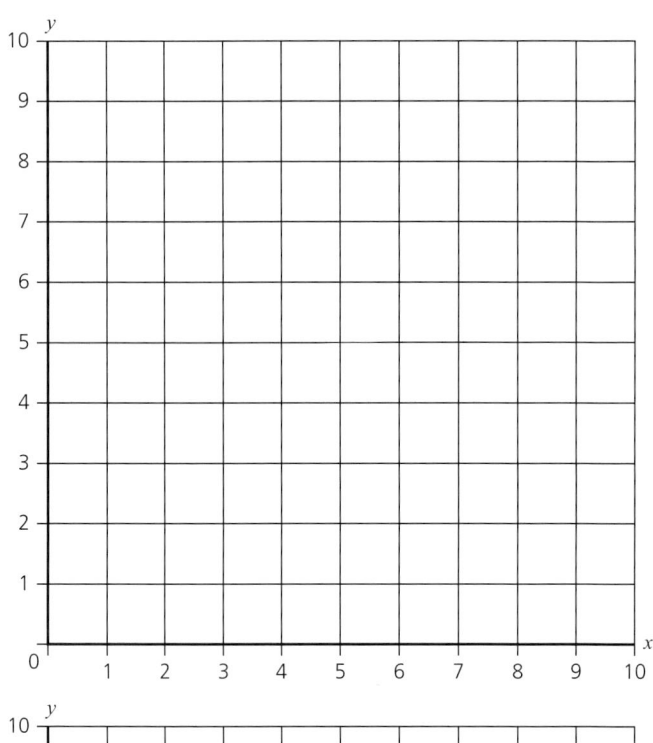

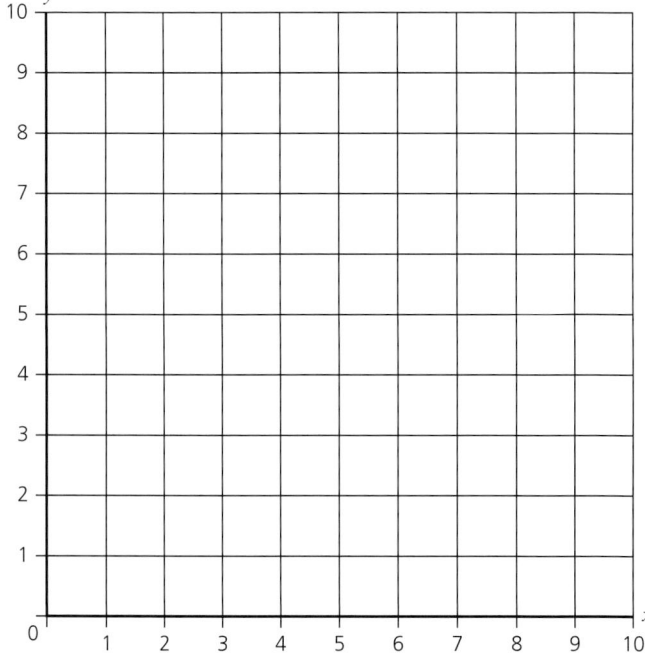

Name: _____ Class: _____ Date: _____

Worksheet for Exercise 8.2

Name: _____ Class: _____ Date: _____

1. First write out the results in the 3 times table. Then double those results to build the 6 times table. Finally, treble the results in the 3 times table to build the 9 times table.

3 times table		6 times table		9 times table	
0 × 3 =		0 × 6 =		0 × 9 =	
1 × 3 =		1 × 6 =		1 × 9 =	
2 × 3 =		2 × 6 =		2 × 9 =	
3 × 3 =		3 × 6 =		3 × 9 =	
4 × 3 =		4 × 6 =		4 × 9 =	
5 × 3 =		5 × 6 =		5 × 9 =	
6 × 3 =		6 × 6 =		6 × 9 =	
7 × 3 =		7 × 6 =		7 × 9 =	
8 × 3 =		8 × 6 =		8 × 9 =	
9 × 3 =		9 × 6 =		9 × 9 =	
10 × 3 =		10 × 6 =		10 × 9 =	
11 × 3 =		11 × 6 =		11 × 9 =	
12 × 3 =		12 × 6 =		12 × 9 =	

2. First, write out the results in the 4 times table and the 6 times table. Then either double the 6 times table or treble the 4 times table to build the 12 times table.

4 times table		6 times table		12 times table	
0 × 4 =		0 × 6 =		0 × 12 =	
1 × 4 =		1 × 6 =		1 × 12 =	
2 × 4 =		2 × 6 =		2 × 12 =	
3 × 4 =		3 × 6 =		3 × 12 =	
4 × 4 =		4 × 6 =		4 × 12 =	
5 × 4 =		5 × 6 =		5 × 12 =	
6 × 4 =		6 × 6 =		6 × 12 =	
7 × 4 =		7 × 6 =		7 × 12 =	
8 × 4 =		8 × 6 =		8 × 12 =	
9 × 4 =		9 × 6 =		9 × 12 =	
10 × 4 =		10 × 6 =		10 × 12 =	
11 × 4 =		11 × 6 =		11 × 12 =	
12 × 4 =		12 × 6 =		12 × 12 =	

Worksheet for Exercise 8.3

Name: _____ Class: _____ Date: _____

1 Write in all the products that you already know. Finally, fill in any gaps by counting on.

7 times table	
0 × 7 =	
1 × 7 =	
2 × 7 =	
3 × 7 =	
4 × 7 =	
5 × 7 =	
6 × 7 =	
7 × 7 =	
8 × 7 =	
9 × 7 =	
10 × 7 =	
11 × 7 =	
12 × 7 =	

2 Write in all the answers that you already know. Finally, fill in any gaps by counting on.

11 times table	
0 × 11 =	
1 × 11 =	
2 × 11 =	
3 × 11 =	
4 × 11 =	
5 × 11 =	
6 × 11 =	
7 × 11 =	
8 × 11 =	
9 × 11 =	
10 × 11 =	
11 × 11 =	
12 × 11 =	

Worksheet for Exercise 8.5

Name: _____ Class: _____ Date: _____

Complete these inverse tables for the 6, 7, 9, 11 and 12 times tables. They are not in order so, if you are not sure, you might want to check the times tables that you completed earlier.

6 inverse times table	
0 ÷ 6 =	
60 ÷ 6 =	
18 ÷ 6 =	
72 ÷ 6 =	
66 ÷ 6 =	
54 ÷ 6 =	
6 ÷ 6 =	
12 ÷ 6 =	
24 ÷ 6 =	
48 ÷ 6 =	
42 ÷ 6 =	
36 ÷ 6 =	
30 ÷ 6 =	

7 inverse times table	
7 ÷ 7 =	
77 ÷ 7 =	
21 ÷ 7 =	
35 ÷ 7 =	
14 ÷ 7 =	
42 ÷ 7 =	
28 ÷ 7 =	
63 ÷ 7 =	
70 ÷ 7 =	
0 ÷ 7 =	
56 ÷ 7 =	
84 ÷ 7 =	
49 ÷ 7 =	

9 inverse times table	
18 ÷ 9 =	
45 ÷ 9 =	
27 ÷ 9 =	
9 ÷ 9 =	
36 ÷ 9 =	
0 ÷ 9 =	
63 ÷ 9 =	
90 ÷ 9 =	
81 ÷ 9 =	
99 ÷ 9 =	
72 ÷ 9 =	
108 ÷ 9 =	
54 ÷ 9 =	

11 inverse times table	
22 ÷ 11 =	
11 ÷ 11 =	
66 ÷ 11 =	
55 ÷ 11 =	
0 ÷ 11 =	
99 ÷ 11 =	
33 ÷ 11 =	
88 ÷ 11 =	
44 ÷ 11 =	
121 ÷ 11 =	
77 ÷ 11 =	
132 ÷ 11 =	
110 ÷ 11 =	

12 inverse times table	
24 ÷ 12 =	
60 ÷ 12 =	
12 ÷ 12 =	
36 ÷ 12 =	
72 ÷ 12 =	
0 ÷ 12 =	
48 ÷ 12 =	
120 ÷ 12 =	
96 ÷ 12 =	
108 ÷ 12 =	
144 ÷ 12 =	
84 ÷ 12 =	
132 ÷ 12 =	

Worksheet for Activity 9

Name: _____ Class: _____ Date: _____

Use the lattice method to work these out.

1 47 × 6

4 143 × 5

2 75 × 7

5 426 × 4

3 69 × 8

6 296 × 9

Name: _____ Class: _____ Date: _____

Now make up some for yourself.

Worksheet for Exercise 14.2

Name: _____ Class: _____ Date: _____

Draw each time on an analogue clock face.

1 (a) 8 o'clock   (b) Half past 4   (c) Quarter to 6   (d) Quarter past 10

2 (a) 10 minutes past 5   (b) 20 minutes to 11   (c) 20 minutes past 9   (d) 10 minutes to 2

3 (a) 5 minutes past 10   (b) 25 minutes to 6   (c) 5 minutes to 3   (d) 25 minutes past 8

4 (a) 8 minutes past 5   (b) 22 minutes to 9   (c) 18 minutes past 11   (d) 6 minutes to 7

Worksheet for Exercise 14.3

Name: _____ Class: _____ Date: _____

3 Write each digital clock time as a 'past' or 'to' the hour time and the draw it on the analogue clock face.

(a) 1:15   (c) 7:35   (e) 4:12

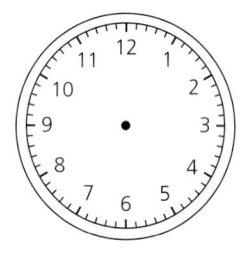

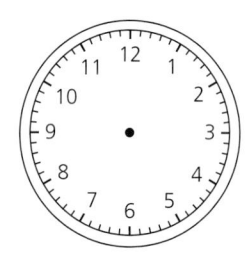

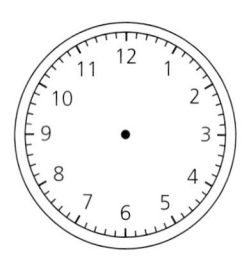

_____   _____   _____

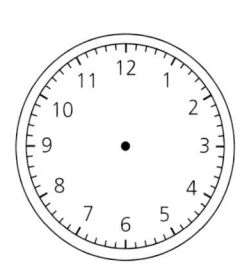

(b) 9:30   (d) 11:55   (f) 2:42

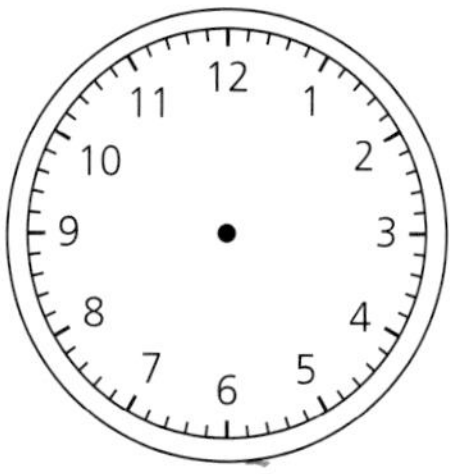

_____   _____   _____

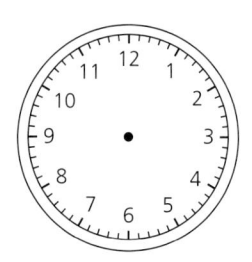

Worksheet for Exercise 14.4

Name: _____ Class: _____ Date: _____

3 (a) 9.43 a.m.   (c) 4.06 a.m.   (e) 12.15 a.m.

(b) 11.32 p.m.   (d) 7.54 p.m.   (f) 12.36 p.m.

4 (a) 11:12   (c) 12:46   (e) 09:23

(b) 20:43   (d) 16:12   (f) 00:12

Worksheet for Activity 14

Name: _____ Class: _____ Date: _____

1

Month	Start day	End day	Difference
January			
February			
March			
April			
May			
June			
July			
August			
September			
October			
November			
December			

Copy and complete the sentences below.

2   I notice that for months with 31 days the end day is _____ days after the start day.

3   I notice that for months with 30 days the end day is _____ days after the start day.

4   This is because _____

_____

_____

Worksheet for Exercise 15.3

Name: _____ Class: _____ Date: _____

Copy each pair of rectangles and colour them to show each pair of equivalent fractions.

1 $\dfrac{1}{4} = \dfrac{2}{8}$

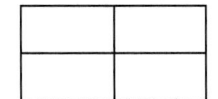

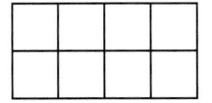

2 $\dfrac{1}{2} = \dfrac{3}{6}$

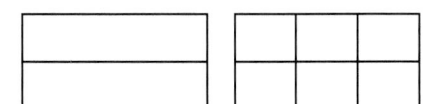

3 $\dfrac{1}{5} = \dfrac{2}{10}$

4 $\dfrac{2}{5} = \dfrac{4}{10}$

5 $\dfrac{3}{5} = \dfrac{6}{10}$

6 $\dfrac{1}{3} = \dfrac{2}{6}$

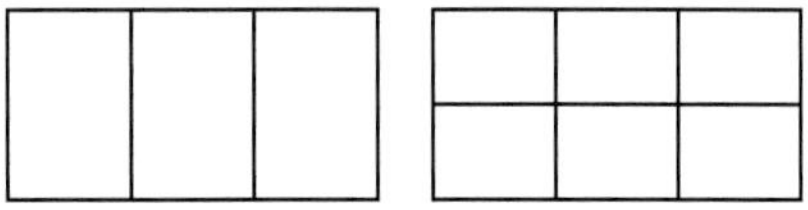

7 $\dfrac{2}{3} = \dfrac{4}{6}$

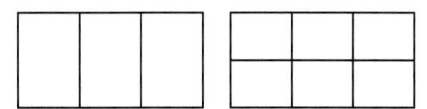

8 $\dfrac{2}{3} = \dfrac{6}{9}$

9 $\dfrac{3}{8} = \dfrac{9}{24}$

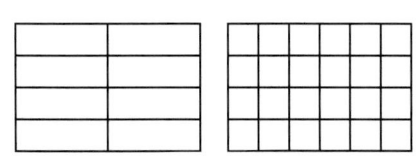

10 $\dfrac{5}{12} = \dfrac{10}{24}$

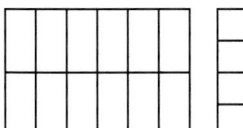

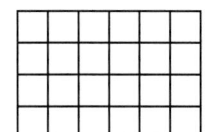

Name: _____ Class: _____ Date: _____

11 Copy and complete this table to show the family of sixths and their equivalent fractions in thirds and halves.

sixths	$\frac{1}{6}$	$\frac{2}{6}$	$\frac{3}{6}$	$\frac{4}{6}$	$\frac{5}{6}$
thirds	$\frac{\Box}{3}$			$\frac{\Box}{3}$	
halves			$\frac{\Box}{2}$		

12 Copy and complete this table to show the family of eighths and their equivalent fractions in quarters and halves.

eighths	$\frac{1}{8}$	$\frac{2}{8}$	$\frac{3}{8}$	$\frac{4}{8}$	$\frac{5}{8}$	$\frac{6}{8}$	$\frac{7}{8}$
quarters		$\frac{\Box}{4}$				$\frac{\Box}{4}$	
halves				$\frac{\Box}{2}$			

13 Copy and complete this table to show the family of tenths and their equivalent fractions in fifths and halves.

tenths	$\frac{1}{10}$	$\frac{2}{10}$	$\frac{3}{10}$	$\frac{4}{10}$	$\frac{5}{10}$	$\frac{6}{10}$	$\frac{7}{10}$	$\frac{8}{10}$	$\frac{9}{10}$
fifths and halves		$\frac{\Box}{5}$		$\frac{\Box}{5}$	$\frac{\Box}{2}$	$\frac{\Box}{5}$		$\frac{\Box}{5}$	

14 Copy and complete this table to show the family of twelfths and their equivalent fractions.

twelfths	$\frac{1}{12}$	$\frac{2}{12}$	$\frac{3}{12}$	$\frac{4}{12}$	$\frac{5}{12}$	$\frac{6}{12}$	$\frac{7}{12}$	$\frac{8}{12}$	$\frac{9}{12}$	$\frac{10}{12}$	$\frac{11}{12}$
equivalent fractions		$\frac{\Box}{6}$	$\frac{\Box}{4}$	$\frac{\Box}{3}$		$\frac{\Box}{2}$		$\frac{\Box}{3}$	$\frac{\Box}{4}$	$\frac{\Box}{6}$	

Worksheet for Activity – Equivalent squares

Name: _____ Class: _____ Date: _____

Cut of the squares below. Then arrange them so that sides that touch have equivalent fractions. The grey triangle is 'wild' and can match up with any other side.

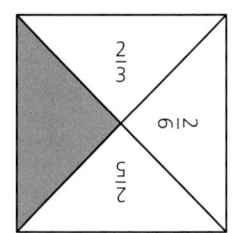

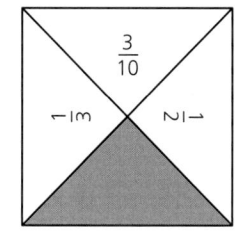

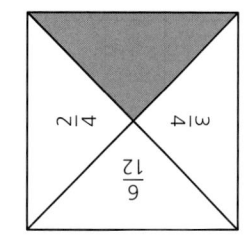

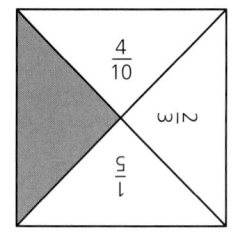

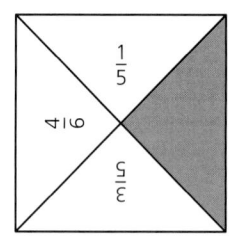

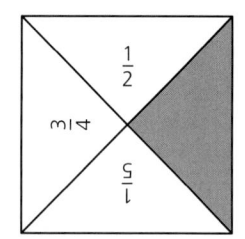

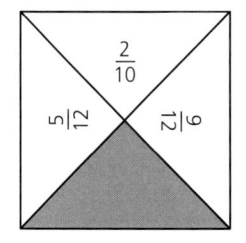

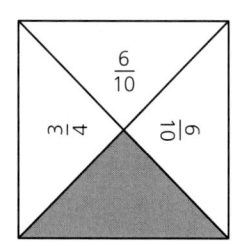

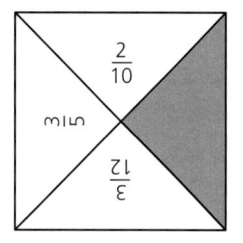

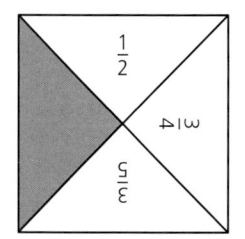

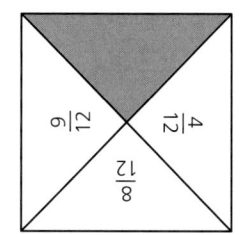

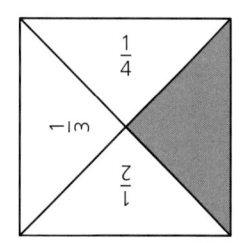

Worksheet for Exercise 14.7

Name: _____ Class: _____ Date: _____

2 (i) Draw hands on an analogue clock to show each of these times.

(ii) All times are a.m. times. Write each of them as a 24-hour clock time.

(a) Quarter to eight

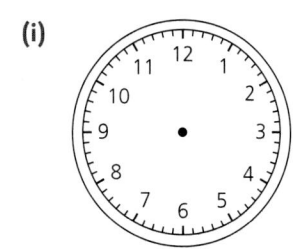

(i)

(ii) _____

(b) Half past three

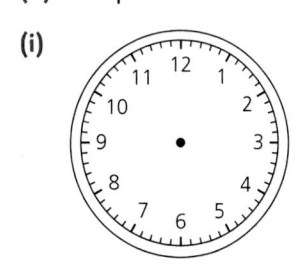

(i)

(ii) _____

(c) Five to eleven

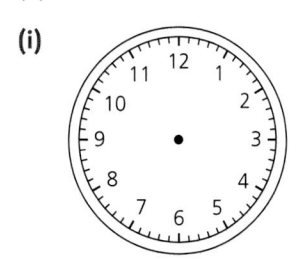

(i)

(ii) _____

(d) Twenty-six minutes past nine

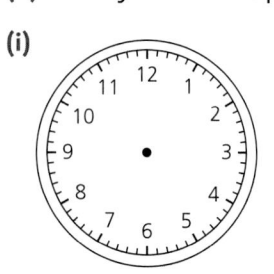

(i)

(ii) _____

(e) Twelve minutes to two

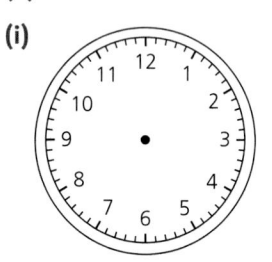

(i)

(ii) _____

(f) Nine minutes past midnight

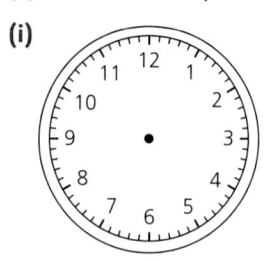

(i)

(ii) _____

Worksheet for Activity 17

Name: _____ Class: _____ Date: _____

Preparation

Cut out a set of dominoes.

Sticking the dominoes onto card first will make them easier to handle.

| $\frac{1}{10}$ | 0.2 | | $\frac{1}{5}$ | 0.4 | | $\frac{3}{10}$ | 0.1 |

| $\frac{2}{5}$ | 0.6 | | $\frac{1}{2}$ | 0.9 | | $\frac{3}{5}$ | 0.5 |

| $\frac{7}{10}$ | 0.8 | | $\frac{4}{5}$ | 0.25 | | $\frac{9}{10}$ | 0.75 |

| $\frac{1}{4}$ | 0.7 | | $\frac{3}{4}$ | 0.3 | | 0.1 | $\frac{1}{2}$ |

| 0.2 | $\frac{3}{10}$ | | 0.3 | $\frac{4}{5}$ | | 0.4 | $\frac{1}{4}$ |

Worksheet for Exercise 20.6

Name: _____ Class: _____ Date: _____

1   Put a small, neat cross on the grid to mark the co-ordinates of each point you are given. Use the eight compass directions to describe the shortest route between the given points.

(a) From P to (4, 8)
(b) From P to (8, 4)
(c) From P to (8, 14)
(d) From P to (14, 8)
(e) From P to (14, 2)
(f) From P to (4, 12)
(g) From P to (15, 15)
(h) From P to (0, 0)
(i) From P to (7, 12)
(j) From P to (9, 5)

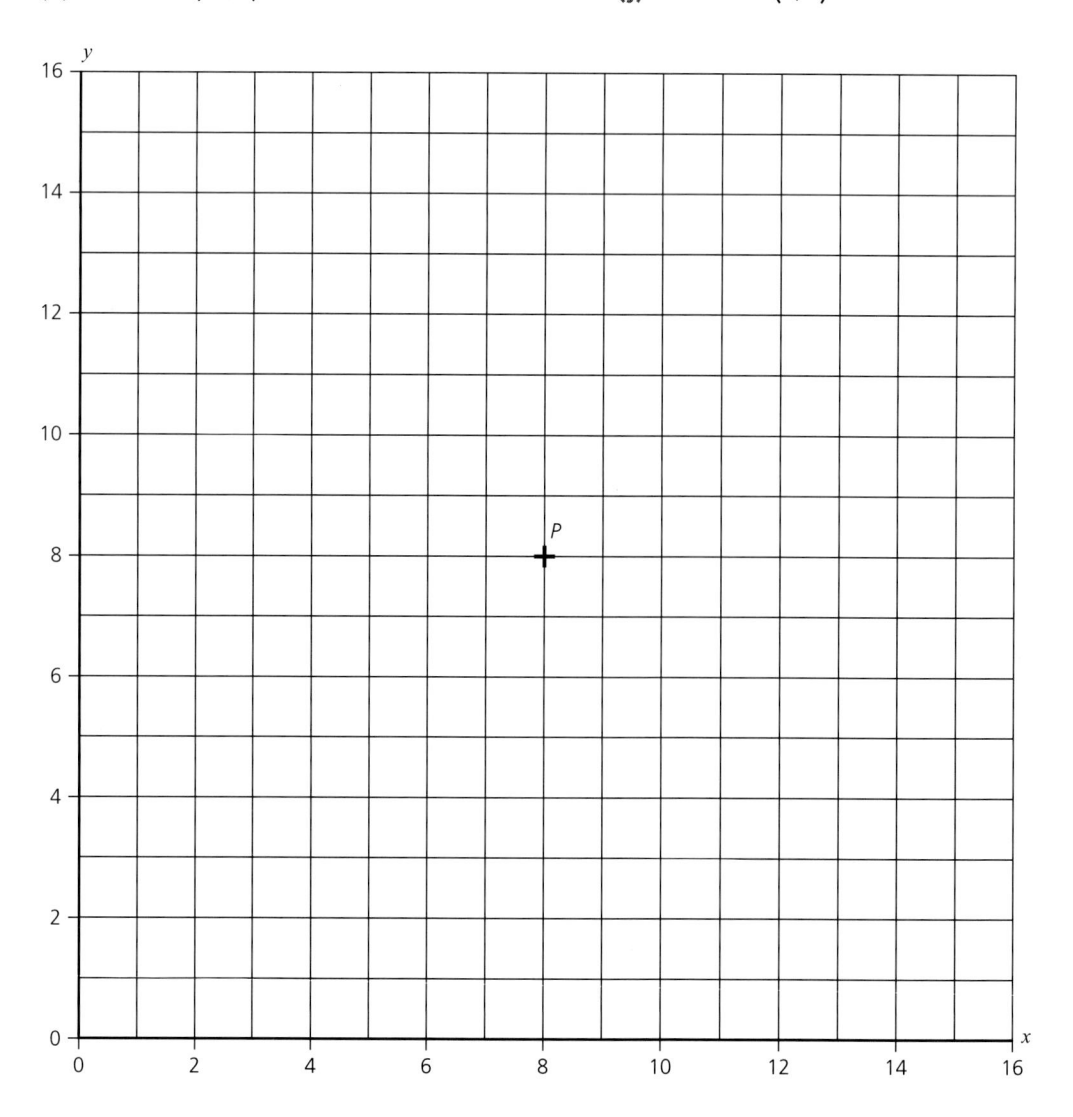

Worksheet for Activity 20

Name: _____ Class: _____ Date: _____

You are going to draw some shapes using the hour positions or points on the clock face.

For each shape, follow these steps.
- Start at 12 and move in a clockwise direction.
- Join the hour points with straight lines.
- Stop when you start repeating yourself.

Shape 1   Join the hours in order.   12 → 1 → 2 → 3 → ...

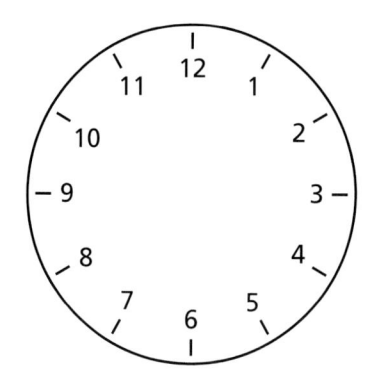

Shape 2   Join the hours, missing 1 hour each time.   12 → 2 → 4 → 6 → ...

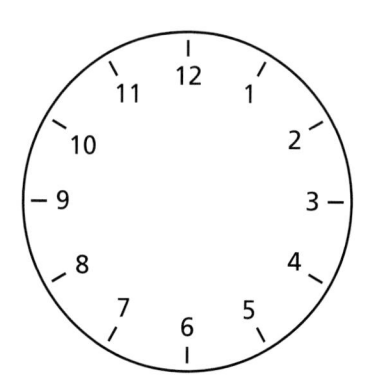

Name: _____ Class: _____ Date: _____

Shape 3 Join the hours, missing 2 hours each time.   12 → 3 → 6 → ...

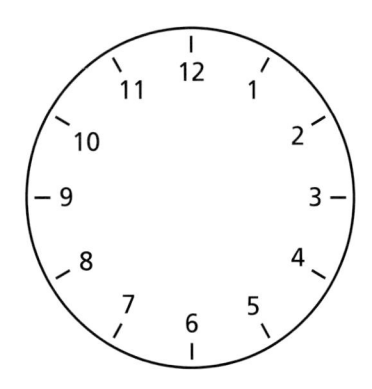

Shape 4 Join the hours, missing 3 hours each time.   12 → 4 → ...

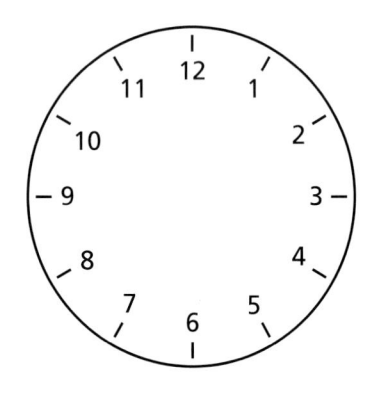

Shape 5 Join the hours, missing 4 hours each time.   12 → 5 → 10 → 3 → ...

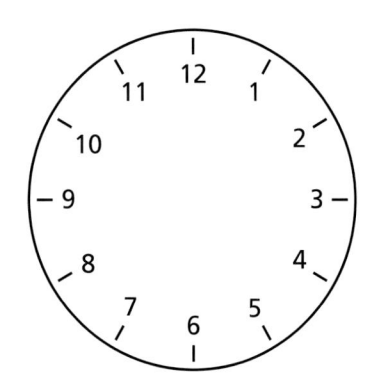

Name: _____ Class: _____ Date: _____

Shape 6 Join the hours, missing 5 hours each time. 12 → 6 → ...

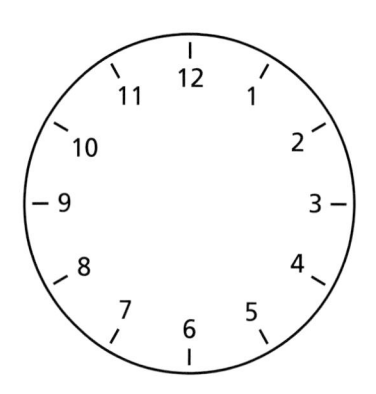

Shape 7 Join the hours, missing 6 hours each time. 12 → 7 → 2 → 9 → ...

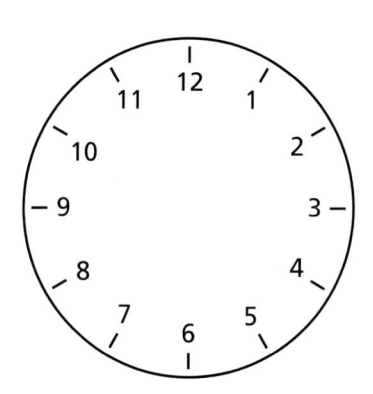

What do you notice?

_____

_____

What will the next patterns be?

_____

_____

Worksheet for Exercise 22.3

Name: _____ Class: _____ Date: _____

On the scales below, draw arrows to mark the numbers A, B, and C.

1 A = 500, B = 900 and C = 350

2 A = 400, B = 700 and C = 150

3 A = 500, B = 250 and C = 800

4 A = 300, B = 600 and C = 750

5 A = 0.5, B = 0.1 and C = 0.65

6 A = 0.2, B = 0.7 and C = 0.85

7 A = 0.5, B = 0.25 and C = 0.9

8 A = 0.3, B = 0.6 and C = 0.75

Worksheet for Summary Exercise 22.4

Name: _____ Class: _____ Date: _____

2 Copy each scale and mark the numbers A, B, and C with arrows.

(a) A = 0.6, B = 0.75 and C = 0.25

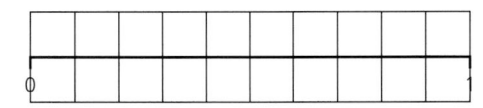

(b) A = 0.5, B = 0.4 and C = 0.2

(c) A = 1, B = 6 and C = 8.5

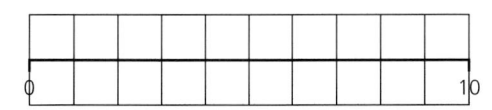

(d) A = 5, B = 7 and C = 2.5

(e) A = 20, B = 60 and C = 85

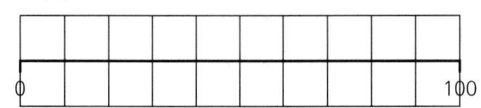

(f) A = 50, B = 75 and C = 10

(g) A = 300, B = 800 and C = 450

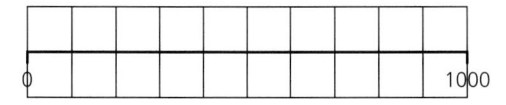

(h) A = 500, B = 250 and C = 750

Worksheet for Exercise 24.2

Name: _____ Class: _____ Date: _____

1 The school netball team played 16 matches during the term. These are the numbers of goals it scored in the 16 matches.

| 2 | 0 | 4 | 1 | 2 | 5 | 6 | 4 |
| 1 | 0 | 5 | 3 | 0 | 2 | 4 | 4 |

(a) Complete the frequency table.

Number of goals	Tally	Frequency
0		
1		
2		
3		
4		
5		
6		
Total		

(b) Show the information from your completed frequency table in a bar chart.

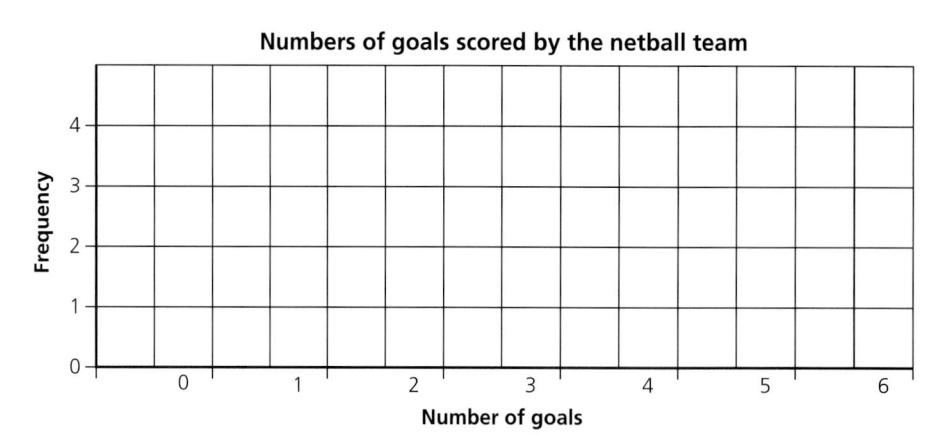

Numbers of goals scored by the netball team

(c) In 4 matches they shot 4 goals. How many goals were scored altogether in those 4 matches?
_____

(d) What was the total number of goals scored? _____

Name: _____ Class: _____ Date: _____

2 At break, children have a choice of fruit to eat: Apple (A), Banana (B), Melon (M), Orange (O) or Strawberries (S). The school cook monitored what was chosen. This is what she recorded.

B	A	O	S	B	M	O	S	S	A
S	B	B	O	M	M	A	S	M	O
M	O	B	S	S	B	A	B	O	M
O	B	B	S	S	O	S	M	A	S
S	M	M	O	S	A	B	B	S	O

(a) Complete the frequency table.

Type of fruit	Tally	Frequency
Apple		
Banana		
Melon		
Orange		
Strawberries		
	Total	

(b) Show the information from your completed frequency table in a bar chart.

Fruits chosen at break time

(bar chart with Frequency axis 0–16 and Type of fruit axis: Apple, Banana, Melon, Orange, Strawberries)

(c) Which was the least popular fruit? _____

(d) What do you think the school cook should do with her survey results?
_____

Worksheet for Exercise 24.4

Name: _____ Class: _____ Date: _____

1 I planted a bean and then measured the height of the plant, in centimetres, every 2 days as it grew. These are my results.

Day	0	2	4	6	8	10	12	14
Height (cm)	0	3	14	17	20	22	24	24

(a) and (b) Plot a + for the height of the bean plant on each day and then join up the points.

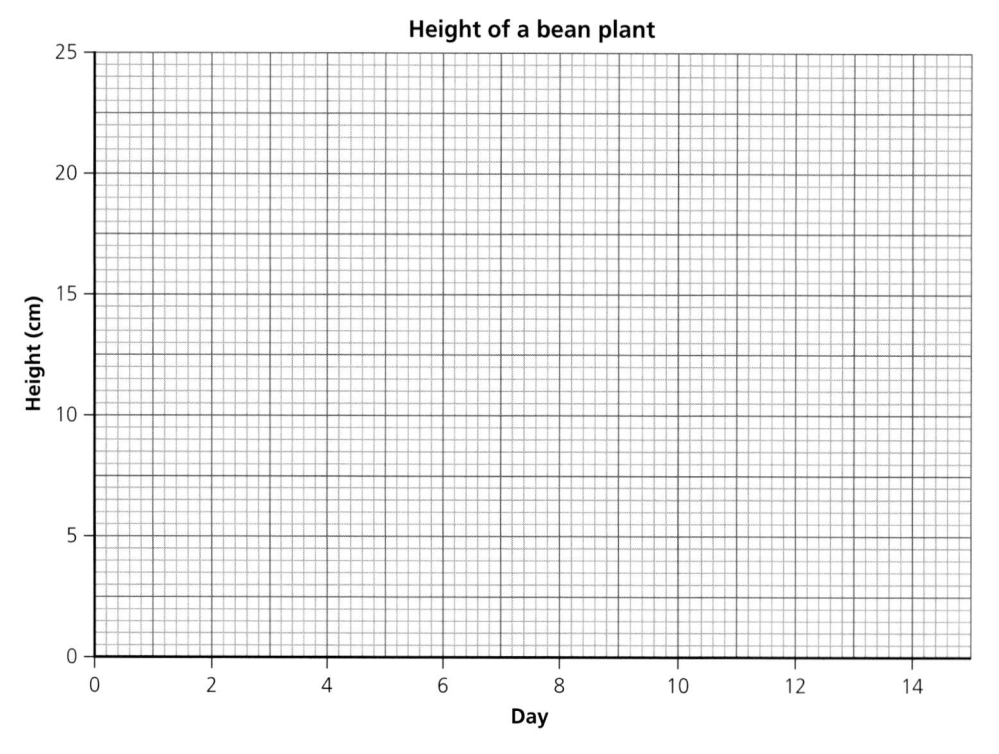

Height of a bean plant

(c) In which two-day period did my plant grow most quickly?

_____

Name: _____ Class: _____ Date: _____

2 I recorded the temperature in my garden every hour from 11a.m. to 5p.m. These are the results.

Time	11a.m	12 noon	1p.m.	2p.m.	3p.m.	4p.m.	5p.m.
Temp (°C)	28°	26°	24°	25°	28°	29°	30°

(a) and (b) Plot a + for the temperature each hour and then join up the points.

Temperature in my garden

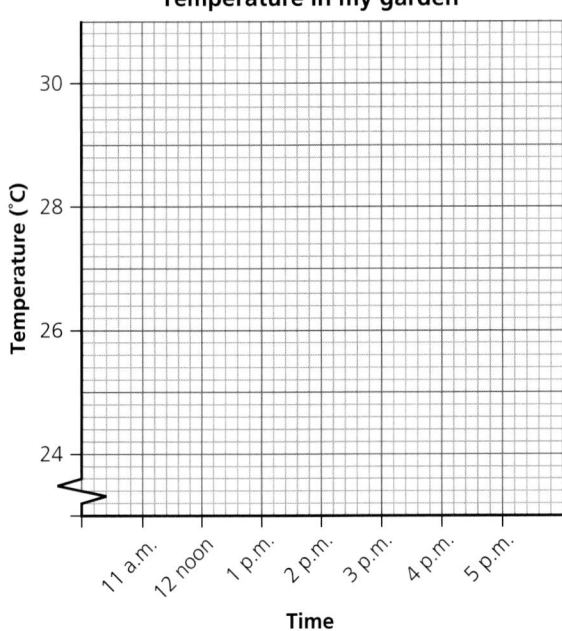

(c) Between which two hours did the temperature increase most?
_____

Name: _____ Class: _____ Date: _____

3 A postman recorded how far he was from the post office every hour. These are his results.

Time	6 a.m.	7 a.m.	8 a.m.	9 a.m.	10 a.m.	11 a.m.	noon	1 p.m.
Distance (km)	0	3	6	9	11	9	5	0

(b) Plot a + for the distance each hour and then join up the points.

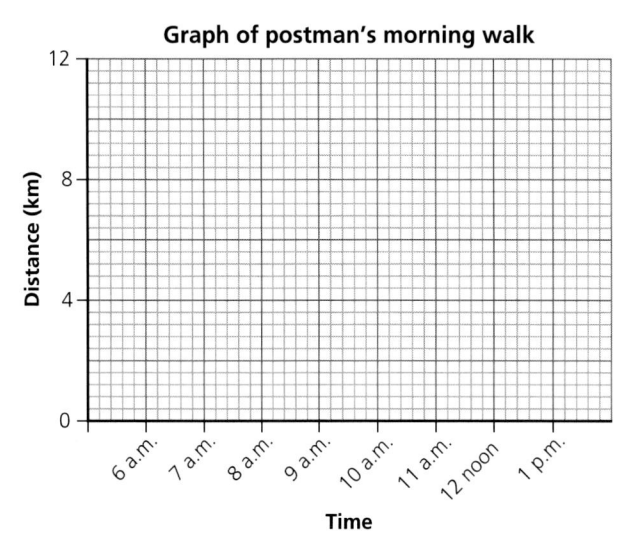

Graph of postman's morning walk

(Graph with Distance (km) on y-axis from 0 to 12, and Time on x-axis from 6 a.m. to 1 p.m.)

(c) At what time was the postman furthest from the post office?
_____

(d) Between what times did he travel fastest?
_____

(e) Why do you think that was?
_____

Name: _____ Class: _____ Date: _____

4 These are company sales one week last June.

Day of week	Mon	Tues	Wed	Thurs	Fri	Sat	Sun
Sales in £ thousands	10	20	45	105	125	145	95

(b) Plot a + for the sales each day and then join up the points.

Company sales one week last June

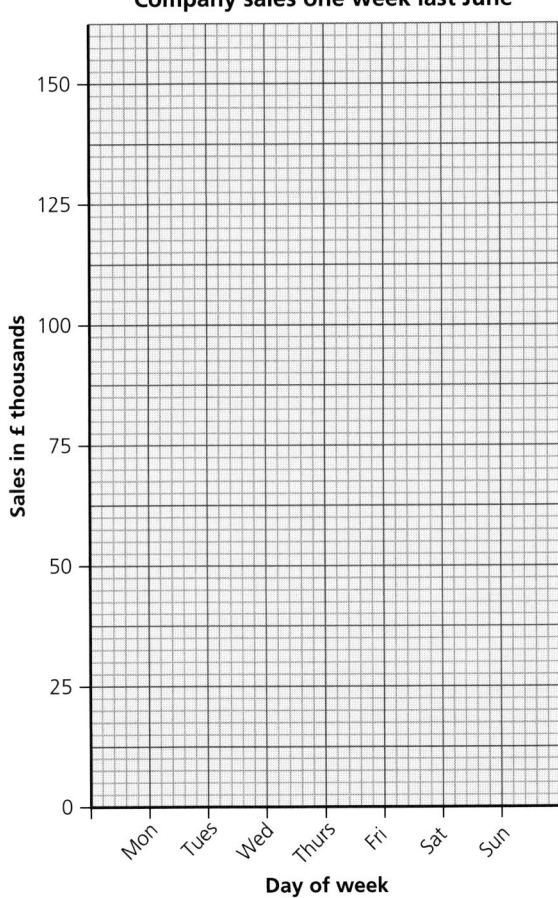

(c) On which day did the company make the biggest sales?
_____

(d) For how many days were the sales more than a hundred thousand pounds?
_____